Critical Sexual Theory

Second Edition

New York, NY
United States of America
© 2025 Baruch Menache
Published by McWest & Associates
All rights reserved. 978-1-971928-10-4

Critical Sexual Theory

Sexuality, Consciousness, and the Architecture of the Psyche

Baruch Menache

Introduction

The foundational thinkers within the field of sexuality have outlined the roots of sexual confusion. Although their primary focus rested on subjective experience, such considerations may be extended to the communal level. When subjective experiences converge, they form a single, intertwined experience; thus, a communal experience may be regarded as a unified social construct composed of all participating individuals. Freud's conclusions were not the result of an obsession with sexuality nor a disdain for it; rather, they emerged from a careful examination of the issues within subjective experience, with the aim of understanding their fundamental nature.[1]

Accusations of bias against Freud necessitate the identification of explicit evidence within his writings and a critical assessment of whether such bias undermines his conclusions. To label Freud as a reductionist presupposes an understanding of a more comprehensive framework of human experience than the one he presented per the lens of sexuality. Dismissing a theoretical perspective as reductive without first demonstrating familiarity with a more nuanced alternative is intellectually dishonest (de Beauvoir 2011, 52).[2]

Moreover, uncritical acceptance of scholarly critiques, without engaging in independent study, reflects a failure in rigorous academic inquiry. Recognizing one's own epistemic limitations concerning sexuality is essential when addressing such a complex and sensitive subject.

Sexuality functions ambiguously. Intellectual inquiry can lead to conclusions that prove more detrimental to the sexual well-being than ignorance. On the other hand, individuals deeply troubled by the nature of sexuality may seek **a** deeper understanding through such study. It is common to encounter derogatory characterizations of Freud using terms he himself introduced, e.g., narcissist. Such reactions reveal a segment of the populace that interprets his theories as degrading to sexuality.

The sexual revolution, for example, could cite the scientific study of sexuality as a justification for dismantling all existing sexual norms. Yet, just as Nietzsche's concept of the Übermensch has been misused to rationalize domination, Freud's ideas can be distorted by those unable to handle abstract theory or unaware of its intellectual origins. This distortion is a common fate of deep intellectual exploration. For the individual who diligently engages with it, enlightenment follows. However, degradation often ensnares the general populace, who struggle with abstract jargon or remain unaware of its intellectual beginnings.

Technology, too, had a vision that was ultimately left at the front door, while only the physical toy was allowed inside.[3] The prevailing inventors dreamed of technology as liberating humanity from governmental constraints, but the usage of technology became automatic, granting rights without purpose or understanding. The sexual revolution was quite similar. Without the intellectual underpinnings, what remained of the theory was simply "more sex"; a narrow vision for the general public. The ambiguous nature has a reversal on the standard individual. Without intellectual understanding of sexuality, sex degrades into dysfunction, much like a culture lacking intellectual foundations degenerates. This was also evident in the South's position on slavery, which lacked solid philosophical argumentation when compared to the North.[4]

The approach taken here is not to find the nature of subjective experience, though such an understanding is appreciated when it emerges from study. The subject of sexuality holds personal significance because it is a natural expression, and the desire is to explore its fundamental principles, purely as a sexual being. Reducing sexual obsessions to an addiction or other such criteria precludes even the simplest exploration of the subject. Intellectual exploration, particularly when one is deeply enmeshed in the struggle, presents a challenge that existentially impacts individuals. For this reason, there is a temptation to seek an easier path, one that dissociates from the issue, choosing instead to consider it a dependence and thereby avoid necessary sexual exploration. Additionally, there is an inherent slight to oneself when, instead of granting the psyche answers to pressing issues, one seeks to circumvent them with something more palatable, both to oneself and society.

The only path to liberation from sexual troubles is through more intellectual study, not less, even if such study uncovers subjects that society may deem abhorrent. The very fact that all historical societies maintained norms that restricted sexuality underscores the importance of this study. It can be surmised from the finality of this text that the specific connection between society and a set of sexual norms is critical. For the time being, it will be stated that if one society liberated childhood sexuality, it is precisely the norm of liberation which stifles the child who does not seek to express their sexuality. When it becomes expected of all children to engage in sexuality, there is still a restraint for the one who doesn't express themselves as such, e.g., the virgin. The social demand compels the child into sexual expression, no less cruel than the social demand which restricts the child. In the society where childhood sexuality is protected, the norm of restricted sexual expression will stifle the child who seeks such.

Either liberation or lack thereof will create sexual restraint on some portion of the populace. The argument that a society can construct itself on neither sexual liberation nor repression is a fundamental misunderstanding of justice. Since someone must be protected contained by the judicial system, wherein should justice be enacted upon? For example, in Pre-Contact Hawaii, where there was no individualistic sexual expression because it was expected of all, sexual dysfunction might not have arisen. However, individuals in such a society would never develop a unique sexual voice. (Diamond, 2023)[5]

—"Individuals of both sexes were expected to initiate and participate in coitus at puberty, although sexual activity, play, instruction, and so forth occurred much earlier. For instance, as part of exploratory play, the young investigated each other's genitals, and young males and females might masturbate each other heterosexually or homosexually. This activity occurred without adult disapproval and was considered an introduction to adulthood" (Diamond).

With such experiences, the societal norm was to relinquish personal ownership of sexuality. Thus, the liberation of sexuality paradoxically becomes its restriction. As will be discussed, the essence of sexuality is partly woven into the fabric of the individuality and partly independent of it. Alongside communal demands for sexual expression, the component of sexual substance that pertains to personhood is severed from the individual's subjective state. This detachment occurs without personal exploration of "letting oneself go" or "keeping for oneself," and this lack of intellectual growth may prove detrimental.

How can one who has never explored their sexuality in their private margins truly explore all other aspects of thought, which are far less tied to subjective experience? Such a society will never achieve the extraordinary human accomplishments of the current tradition, which compelled individuals to wrestle with sexuality in the shadows of societal prohibitions. In later cultural developments, this model evolves into the exploration of intellectual masterpieces in the darkness of society.

The same dilemma arises regarding masculinity and femininity. The judicial system would either protect the feminine from masculine expression, or it would assure the masculine expression of fulfillment, as seen in certain doctrines. This study is motivated by personal sexual confusion, which will guide the journey forward. It is acknowledged that the biases of the author cannot be denied, as they are intrinsic to the subject matter itself. This prejudice is openly stated and is intertwined with the individual's masculinity. Thus, those with a feminine perspective cannot claim that this exploration reflects an "overtly masculine view" since the predisposition is candidly disclosed. It is a partiality that the author does not wish to part with, just as they do not wish to depart from sexual expression itself.

Sexuality must be viewed as an expression requiring assistance to convey it to the forefront of consciousness. This assistance is vital because the nature of sexual experience is concealed within the deep recesses of subjective experience. It remains hidden due to a hesitancy to express itself, as it is unsure of whether it possesses the right to emerge. The ambivalence of sexuality makes it fluid and changing from moment to moment. One side of the equation seeks expression, while the other requires a catalyst to release its vitality. This requirement of a third-party vitality is because sexuality is only a form potential and does not bear the name of actuality. Like a child who is doubtful of their independence, unsure if they have autonomy or if they are dependent on their parents. This substance of sexuality does not know if it is granted independence and thus to be expressed, or if this substance is dependent on its paternal status; the fabric of the person itself.

Expression of sexuality cannot be seen by the same token to other expressions, such as emotions, since sexuality must be looked at as both a derivative of oneself and, coincidentally, as independent of oneself. Emotional expression does not have the attribute of being deeply independent of oneself, nor the attribute of being deeply dependent on oneself. If one is angry, the anger is not completely dependent on the fabric of oneself; the expression naturally manifests itself without any catalyst. Sexuality, on the other hand, does not always express itself with a significant sexual catalyst, e.g., nocturnal penile tumescence. Alternatively, anger cannot be viewed as independent of oneself since it can be defused more easily than a heightened sexual experience.

.

PART ONE: FEMININITY AND MASCULINITY

This work is gender-neutral; the invocation of femininity and masculinity can be applied to any higher life forms in so much as we identify a feminine-masculine dynamic. The structure of femininity and masculinity is being explored for its own sake.

Toward Absolute Femininity

We can imagine a particular feminine disposition which connects to femininity in a manner that creates the experience of absolute femininity. To be available to the environment with its unique suppositions, one which does not interfere with the availability in the present moment despite the incoming material. Even as this seems contradictory, since a supposition of any kind would automatically withdraw oneself from the availability to receive all which the environment offers, thereby working an interplay to which the present moment is filled with suppositions. Although in the eventful aspect of the present moment, they would be fully available in the entirety of their persona, to which some will be filtered in regards to the suppositions and others will be extended to any sort of reception.

One will get the sense of something present, yet it will prove to not be intrusive to the interaction. The slight supposition only produces a more elaborate form of reception and does not derail a newfound continuity beyond its particular vitality. The suppositions are present to service a higher degree or form of femininity and not to evade the risk-prone femininity by means of protection. Without the suppositions, the resulting femininity is either bland to the waving environment or too complex for appropriate attunement in respect to the depth of the environment. This profile is one which is to be termed 'perfect' femininity in the sense of it being totally available whilst containing alongside a certain context to distill and interact with the environment in a fanciful fashion.

To note the risks of femininity to which perfect femininity is difficult to come by, we must say a few words. The risks are found to be the exposure of the environment without any mechanism to halt the flow of information. This is not reception per se as this accounts for the limited exposure in reference to things pertaining to masculinity. The rest of personhood is not in respect to these aspects of analysis and can very well be contrary to all of our propositions. This is pertaining to the feminine aspect, to which it finds its vitality in relation to a masculine interface. We are not referring to social beings and rather to elements of experience, so that a masculine environment can excite the feminine disposition without any human aspect to this analysis. The risk of femininity is only in the occasion of dominant masculinity, for if either enervated or nonexistent, the feminine experience ceases to be relevant. When the occasion is a form of directed masculinity, the risk becomes a profound engagement with the existential perspective for which the masculine partakes.

For example, if one were to engage with derogatory suppositions from the outset, it wouldn't be counted as masculine from the feminine perspective. However, when entangled with respectful masculinity to prove ample for feminine concern, which then takes the turn towards an existential perspective which does not highlight further human flourishing and surely feminine vitality, the feminine disposition will be compelled to follow that narrative. The normal safety measures in place for such deception is a keen feminine focus which takes note of the initial impressions to corroborate genuine masculinity from a portrayal of such. When it is genuine, the masculine disposition which is deemed honorary is filled with relationship material and noble frameworks that disallow a plunge into emptiness, to which only a habitat of non-relationship material would produce.

Another risk to be had is the masculine fixation with a particular feminine expression, with the assumption that within the peculiar feminine object can be found all human experience and thus masculine interest. This proves problematic for a feminine beholder who must dispel troubling interactions of the one who contains an assumption to which they can never fulfill. There is nothing that will deter a masculine supposition that assumes to have found all of femininity in a single object, as it is only acting in its masculine interests to follow that aim.

A second disposition is one that is completely available to the environment but does not contain an intricate supposition of any kind, being fully open to the trends and movements of a given time period. Such a disposition is troubled in a natural sense because it will not relinquish femininity, all while finding a remoteness within a given context to receive said femininity. Such a disposition would be an acting agent of trauma and is satisfied with the situation being experienced as the most grand and expansive form of femininity; thus gaining knowledge and intuitions that most persons could not even imagine. This profile is similar to the ancient feminine-leaning character who attuned to witchcraft, magic, and divination, becoming unpredictable in thought but remaining crucial to that layer of reality, or presumed reality, which the social environment requires at intervals. We will call this absolute femininity.

A third disposition is one in which there is mistrust of the environment, assuming it to be too mediocre to fulfill a true experience of femininity. At this level of cynicism has the disposition unavailable in a true feminist sense, instead using the feminist sense to berate the environment as insufficient for material femininity. However, this mistrust is masculine in nature, as it not only provides context for perceiving a given situation but is also an active approach toward situations.

Embodied Connectivity and the Feminine Self

We are to attempt to define femininity in reference to its connection to selfhood and relation to externalities. The feminine self-perception is not centered in its own domain, and even if it doesn't concern itself with a presupposed center, if pressed for an answer it would be retorted as a sort of center in service of external universality. The selfhood that activates itself is a call from that external center.

In terms of its connection, it takes focus on the matter of connection itself and not the substance of the connection. This is because the feminine disposition is to rely on this universal center and to existentially find refuge in being a subsidiary of that system; it highlights the matter of universal connection with the attempt at proposing the connection to be on par with the centrality of the system. When we produce an adequate accounting of the connection from and to the center, we allow the equalization of the center to its subsidiaries.

This is the existential situation; however, the feminine disposition does not interact with such matters as it merely addresses the inadequacy of the situation. Rather most of its vitality is focused on the connection itself, in whatever form it takes. To highlight the connective aspect of nature it must apply all of its existential dynamism to attend to the sensitive details that make up that connection. The major factor of connection is the reason for having two points interact and this is made possible by mirroring a form of selfhood with the intent of interaction. This does not exemplify selfhood as its innate state but as a specific form that applies a certain element of absolute selfhood with a reflective function that will emulate upon the possible interacting aspects.

An important aspect of this equation is that the connectivity is embodied as if it were an entity of itself. There is a certain humility that comes along with this because connectivity does not appear to be a substance. This relies on the interaction for which the substance is manifesting and thus we can attribute the start of the process, the connective layer, to be the foundational element which would ascribe it as concrete. Whatever aspect of personhood is not embodied in the connectivity will not enjoy the ascription of perpetuating substance; thus being equal or greater than it.

Already we are met with an inconsistency as to why the disposition must take the role of the connection and not attend to the connection as it were, without a mirroring selfhood for connectivity purposes. The ability to attend to connection will only grant the experience of connection and would only postulate further that the feminine disposition is a non-center who is granted a depth of connection.

Instead, by embodying an aspect of the connection, the disposition will enjoy the entire state of existential personhood as the actual connection, and this allows for the sensibility of being center-like. The vulnerability of such an approach is that the disposition relies on an external element which participates at the end of that projection. When there is no meeting, the disposition does not retrieve the absolute sensibility of embodied connectivity and is thus compelled into existential disarray. For once it appears that the connection is not genuine, the disposition is presumed to be non-center-like and becomes a subsidiary of the larger system.

We may assume that a degree of humility would solve this disparity; however, due to the investment in the process of embodying the connectivity, there is no availability to revert toward being something else. There is the possible choice of following this with conscious deliberation, choosing not to partake in the connectivity, and to instead partake in the hope that the center will seek out the disposition with the agreement that it is a relevant particle of the system, or even center-like. The in-between period, where neither the center has interest, nor the disposition is preparing the embodiment of connectivity, the disposition lays in the existential arena and does not experience a high level of vitality. Such a choice, of choosing a lifestyle of existential disarray, is not practical as a measure. Instead, other methods of distraction, deviation, and repression are employed. They are consistent in two categories: one in relation to embodying connectivity, and the other in reference to center-like interest. The former can be utilized by embodying connectivity which demands interaction through its powerful means. The means that are worked into the embodied connectivity are not participating in that embodiment; they are elements added to the equation, learned from the environment, and will prove successful.

There is no importance given to the notion of highlighting the connectivity, since the actual interaction will not be experienced as embodied connectivity, but rather as a third-party observer who is experiencing the situation. The method is proposed from a third-party vantage point because of the success rate of such means.

However, the embodiments of connectivity do not concern themselves with success rates or manipulation of interactions. This is done irrespective of success, for it only concerns highlighting the connectivity and not upon the point of connection waiting on the other side. When the interaction point takes center focus, the disposition will no longer be able to experience a center-like state in service of that interaction. This shortcut to the meeting of the interaction proves to demote the position from which the entire enterprise begins.

Another method that may be used is to presume center-interest by following a pathway which produces such in abundance. By following this path, through which the center pays heed to the disposition and proposes an agreement to its relevance, it still will not be experienced in absoluteness. For the interest is not concerned with this specific disposition, since the context that led to the meeting, and thus the existential agreement, has been mediated through many elements which allow the interaction to exist. These elements, for instance, work, are the primary factors that continue the relationship and do not contain a genuine center of interest.

To satisfy the interaction, it must meet an existential criterion. If the recognition of the connectivity is general and not oriented in a very specific manner, it will recognize the connectivity in a universal sense and not in an individual sense. Even as the disposition has placed the entire personhood toward the exposure of connectivity, specific and individualistic, the interaction from the environment is one of non-deliberate recognition. The satisfaction meets the requirement by a certain recognition; it does not, however, please the existential layer that has risked such embodiment.

Dynamic Between Masculine and Feminine Dispositions

To partake in complete integration of masculine and feminine, the feminine disposition must reflect the extraction capsule of the masculine attention that cannot be seen at an external point. The reflection must appear mystifying when viewed from the outside, as if unclear of the circumstance that occurs before them. Such reflection, similar to the physical reality of reflective material, in which each angle is a new perception of the circumstance. To perform such a reflection requires the knowledge of each possible viewpoint per its capacity.

The availability of reflection is both the solution and the problem for further integration. Because reflection is incumbent upon reciprocity between the object of reflection and reflective material, it becomes a suitable habitat for stimulation according to the infinite points of reflection that are possible. Almost as if we consider the personification of the mirror to be experiencing a demand that removes itself from the equation.

If the mirror had any sort of prerogative against the continuing points of reflection it would become a failed source of absolute reflection. On the other side of the spectrum we have a mirror that continuously moves from one reflection to another, so as not to abide by any sort of conscious deliberation of its substance. It is not safe enough as an entity that both performs a restrictive sense and reflection of absoluteness.

Another source external to the mirror must abide by a different set of rules in which it both retrieves certain reflective material and distributes parameters to its ongoing force. When viewing oneself in the mirror, one becomes attached to prior conceptual understandings meant to be seen through it. The cost of absolute reflection, in this case, the mirror, is that it always comes at the expense of a conceptual bridge toward the material. A sophisticated sentiment toward the material would, in turn, arise from crude reflective material. While an open-platform concept allows for truer sensibility toward reflective material; that openness comes with the cost of a lack of specificity about whatever is being exposed.

To imbue a strong sense of masculinity requires questioning whatever is proposed. It involves actively engaging in the recognition that one is not experiencing absolute reflection and is mostly bound by concepts built upon other concepts. There is a belief that the true essence of the feminine experience is more closely connected to nature and offers greater potential for insight from whatever concept arises in the moment. The masculine disposition, on the other hand, recognizes that it has never been exposed to self-reflection in such intricate detail, unencumbered by the intellectual baggage that dictates how it should be understood. This is the sense of pain without prior beliefs about or against it, a pain that reflects back onto itself, delving into its depth of humanism.

Masculinity lacks a humanistic exposure that would allow for an undefined experience of selfhood. It does not know how the arm feels beyond the presupposition of its function. If it were to reflect on the arm without the behavioral attachments that define its effect, it would only encounter an earlier stage of the production process. To experience the arm firsthand as a humanistic phenomenon is a privilege not afforded to the masculine position. It does not know the arm as a mirrored angle of reflection in its infinite forms. For the masculine form, the arm does not reflect because any interactive interest that exists is dutifully bound as a component of a system.

For the feminine experience, the arm is an infinite reflective device of experience, just as a mirror reflects light. This does not mean the feminine experience understands the arm as an infinite measure, but it does mean that it is available to continue its humanistic reflection concerning its substructure. We specifically use the term "humanistic" because it refers to the potency of the elaborated human form, which is most reflective toward the arm. While reflection points can vary across the spectrum, the feminine form is naturally predisposed to more intense forms of *light*. What defines a more potent form of *light* is that it encompasses prior versions of its already finalized product.

This is why the feminine disposition proposes a futuristic human form, it reflects toward the ultimate, conceivable reflection of the human form. Though, there is a limit to the reflection, according to parameters dictated by the environment. Theoretically, the feminine form should espouse the ultimate human form, as it reflects itself into that infinite dimension.

However, the environmental hazards of limitations and expectations demote the feminine form, causing it to lose its infinite stature in order to partake in true social reciprocity.

We could argue that the feminine form, having reached absolute reflection, is unavailable for dynamic exchange in the social realm. It cannot dynamically change because it has lost the inclination to reciprocate from a dimension that cannot relate to whatever is being proposed on the other side of its reflective habitat. It will enjoy, and we use "joy" in the sense of enjoining, the reciprocity of its reflective behavior, as it provides a sense of stability within the infinite measure. The dynamic exchange is a masculine parameter that disrupts the reflective experience, allowing the feminine disposition to behold the seat of humanness and its participation.

Absolute feminine reflection will detach from merging with material in dynamic exchange, and as a result, will not engage with the sense of reflection that the environment interacts with. This detachment leads to a loss of will to continue the reflective propagation, as the mirror reflects only when there is a reflective quality inherent in the material.

What has failed the feminine disposition, which chooses reflection that goes unrecognized in the societal realm, is the loss of sociality, not femininity. The feminine character is not a social potency, just as the mirror does not socialize with the viewer. It offers an objective reflection, disregarding the sensibilities that arise from interaction. Femininity is a force of nature that, under the influence of consciousness, transforms into self-reflection, with unconscious elements acting as a reflective force. Although everything in nature can be reflected upon, and we may refer to nature as feminine, it is the conscious interaction with that reflection that fully outlines the feminine form.

The feminine form consists of two parts: one is the conscious interaction with the reflection, and the other is the reflective properties inherent in a piece of nature. Not every aspect of nature possesses reflective properties, though we can engage in conscious interaction with all aspects. This level of engagement requires a heightened state of consciousness, beyond the standard mode of interaction. Because the feminine disposition is inherently self-reflective, it offers natural reflective properties while simultaneously engaging in its own conscious interaction with the reflection.

The problem with self-reflection is that it merely fulfills whatever consciousness is seeking; it might be more accurately described as a reflection that validates its own consciousness. It will reflect whatever it seeks, which almost goes beyond the notion of reflection, as it follows a conscious interaction without contrasting it to ultimate reality. The internal notion of consciousness is not a contrasting agent; so, self-reflection becomes two distinct components of the psyche, which are distant in relation to each other, each serving as a form of self-reflection. Yet, within this distance, a logical continuity arises, linking the reflection back to its source within itself. However, the external agent of conscious interaction will be suitable for reflection, as a non-logical continuation. Still, the feminine disposition of self-reflection allows for a bridge to the outside agent, which processes the reflective data for extraction.

If the feminine disposition were to remain idle without conscious self-reflection, the conscious agent would find the reflection more akin to the incumbent nature, one which inherently presumes reflective material. The erudition of the feminine disposition lies in the self-reflection that creates a habitat for conscious surroundings. The external conscious agent finds a pathway to the source of reflection, which, firstly, requires little deliberation since the work has already been done, and secondly, the feminine habitat is in a state of self-reflection, offering both containment and reflection.

While the masculine disposition may offer containment through contextual oversight, having the feminine partake in containment allows for a freedom of loose conscious reflection. It's as though the offering is to reflect with a small dose of consciousness, while feminine containment offers it back in double portions.

We could view this as an unfair dynamic exchange, where the masculine form offers only small amounts of conscious reflection while receiving a greater share of conscious and reflective experience. There is no loss for the masculine form, whereas the feminine form lacks the higher degree of consciousness needed to sustain the endeavor. To address this imbalance, the unspoken rule of the masculine form is to employ a higher form of consciousness than the containment-consciousness for which the feminine form has cultivated.

There are multiple ways in which a form of consciousness can be articulated and employed as a higher form in specific contexts. This is especially true in the realm of vulnerability, where a lower form of consciousness can challenge a more potent one, provided it retains weaknesses that the more potent consciousness has yet to address because the feminine form lacks a strong definition, its vulnerability, the masculine form can use as consciousness, always aligning with the feminine form's containment. In this way, the masculine form is endowed with traits like definition, structure, and discipline.

This becomes the conscious strategy for the feminine form, enabling it to offer higher consciousness, even while maintaining some degree of containment. The feminine form cannot fully integrate these vulnerabilities, as doing so would disrupt its reflective experience. These traits are dynamically opposed, and if one dominates, the other weakens. Thus, the feminine disposition chooses to accept these vulnerabilities in order to continue its conscious pursuit.

This requires the masculine disposition to engage these vulnerabilities, not for the vulnerabilities themselves, but because the feminine lacks them. The developed masculine form will acknowledge these vulnerabilities, not as a part of its own consciousness, but as a means of completing the whole of the relationship.

Masculinity, Femininity, and the Decline of Consciousness

Masculinity can be understood as distinct points contained by a continuous, linear progression, whereas femininity embodies the structure itself, in an ever-moving, perpetual flow. In times of decline, femininity assumes the role of consciousness, maintaining its linear progress until it reaches complete dissolution. This is because femininity is existentially open to reality, even in its most destructive states. Masculine energy, by contrast, loses its vitality and becomes a mere background presence. What remains is an unsatisfied feminine disposition, awaiting either the revitalization of masculinity or the final collapse of consciousness and societal order.

This dynamic exacerbates the situation, as masculine actions, at much lower levels of consciousness, must be received by the feminine disposition due to its inherent availability to any interaction. The overflow of consciousness can be both dramatic and exquisite when masculine energy, even at a lower level, disrupts the system. The feminine disposition does not impede such interactions because, at its core, no other force is stepping forward. If it were to impede them, avoiding lower masculine energy, it would contradict its own essence and begin to decline.

Dynamic Between Masculine and Feminine Dispositions

The core of the feminine disposition lies in its ability to align with the existential availability of its surroundings. When that flow is interrupted, what remains is a nostalgic view that fails to carry consciousness into the future.

To illustrate, imagine a masculine obstruction that prevents interaction, assuming it is offering some form of protection or provision. In this scenario, the blockade functions as the masculine point, intended to allow masculine energy, or existential availability, from the outside to enter the inner space. However, this does not occur because the blockade, situated at a very low point on the continuum, is too detached from existential disarray to be effective. While it may offer temporary placation, it fails to allow any evocative disruption into the inner chambers. Instead, he simply resists everything from the outside, effectively blocking the flow.

As a result, the feminine energy contained by the inner chambers becomes disillusioned with the flow of consciousness, transforming into a nostalgic viewpoint that does not foster any growth for the future. The masculine figure that remains, like the blockade, becomes the only form of reciprocity from the external world. However, this offering is so low on the consciousness continuum that it leads to the complete decline of the feminine disposition. In this way, the feminine energy in the inner chambers aligns with the blockage, losing any further complexity or depth beyond that.

The Dissonance between Feminine Disposition and Masculine Perception

The failure of a feminine disposition manifests in its manic form wherein there is a transient ordeal of environmental reception to the advantage of being a feminine figure. Such femininity is not defined by the manner of reception, and all the psychological interruptions to the poignant pieces being received are ignored, only to take on the role of what is assumed to be feminine, but only for a short while. Later, upon the onset of psychological casualties, the role is stripped from possession, and a true feminine disposition is embodied, yet it does not receive adequately from the environment, leading to the failure of femininity in its truest sense.

Rather than undergoing the painstaking work of developing real femininity, it is easier to become an inconsistent reception of all aspects, only to eventually fall back from the impossibility of maintaining this while keeping one's sanity intact.

Worse still, the masculine disposition will assume that such a feminine disposition exists in real form, responding only to this façade of femininity that seemingly receives everything. Without introspection into the impossibility of maintaining this form, the masculine disposition will take this to be the true form of femininity and will cease to seek the development of true femininity. This creates an incentive to avoid the development of true femininity, because even if the disposition were developed, it would not fall within the masculine sphere of attention, as it does not receive at the normalized level.

The only feminine disposition incentivized to continue developing will be those who recall an intuitive memory of a masculine disposition that can perceive true femininity. They must idolize a version of masculinity that does not readily exist in the present, in order to retain the development of femininity and affirm that it participates in a masculine intervention. This process is difficult, as it requires imagination, with the feminine disposition correlating it to present reality, what it could be or once was, until it becomes a tangible reality in the world.

The alternative is to relinquish the stature of true femininity, as the feminine disposition is directly interacting with the masculine of the current era. The choice is whether true femininity will be lost, or whether, instead, the interaction with the masculine disposition, which contains an intuitive sense, will take precedence.

We might argue for the latter, as there will always be a found masculine disposition that may even emerge from nature itself. We must agree that while nature is the source of personhood, personhood is also the source of the perception of nature. From this, we can surmise that the feminine disposition is inclined to endure within the imaginative realm, which will not disrupt its femininity until the moment when reality coincides with its imagination, transforming into a feminine figure that can engage with righteous masculinity.

Another benefit of this approach is the universal growth that will be commendable to the feminine demand, either for intuition on the part of the masculine disposition or to disallow a dynamic in which a feminine disposition is enthroned in an idolized femininity that cannot be upheld. By having these dispositions rumbling through the environment, the universal masculine disposition will become aware of this choice and will gain consciousness of their continuing sub-optimal interactions. Thus, the imaginative idolized version of the feminine disposition becomes the universal idea of a developed masculine disposition.

When the imagination does not lead to a universal trend of masculinity, the feminine disposition will either give up on proper feminine development or develop a certain hostility toward the universal order. If feminine idolization is not incentivizing the masculine disposition, it must mean that masculinity is willing to forgo feminine sensibility in order to maintain success in sub-optimal interactions. This suggests an exponential increase of the masculine disposition consciously ignoring their intuition about the feminine, so as not to disrupt their perspective and continue receiving feminine interaction.

At this point, the feminine disposition invokes the notion of universal femininity, as opposed to the natural, personal feminine disposition. The natural way of the feminine disposition is to progress toward the developing feminine form that aligns with both the social order and masculine perception. In this case, the universal notion of masculinity becomes merely a metric to the alignment of reality alongside true femininity. When the notion of universal femininity arises, it signals that the masculine perception is not aligned with true femininity. The hope is that, through intuitive feminine imagination, the masculine disposition will redirect its course.

The more this does not occur, the more the feminine disposition will invoke universal femininity in order to unify their efforts and prevent both personal degradation and the degradation of the universal system.

Feminine and Masculine Interactions

The environment is of greater concern to the feminine disposition, as it is the realm that promises the most masculine formations. In contrast, the masculine disposition is more attuned to specific interactions wherever they arise. The environment serves as the most agreeable locale for masculine manifestation. While particular interactions may contain masculine energy, they lack the nuance of the environment because they are singular. This is why feminine word-forms tend to exemplify multiplicity, while masculine forms are more singular. The multiplicity of the feminine makes the environment more receptive to masculine manifestation without diluting a particular masculine disposition.

However, a specific masculine disposition, though serviceable to the feminine, carries a major drawback: it does not offer true masculine representation but rather a version that has been deduced for singular use. The feminine disposition engaged with singular masculinity will be compelled to lose the function of femininity in its appropriation of the absolute masculine and its counterpart. In doing so, it settles into a femininity that responds to this specific masculine endeavor, which, by nature, will always be diluted.

The degradation of the feminine disposition occurs when the environment as a whole is either not appreciated or assumed to be unavailable for experience. Instead of the environment becoming the landscape for discerning masculine tendencies, it is sought out in direct interactions. Specifically defined interactions become the entire framework for understanding the feminine build, making it entirely dependent on masculine dispositions for development. When discrepancies arise within these interactions, the feminine build will advance to address them without pausing to introspect onto what the broader environment offers.

What can be defined here is a feminine disposition that neither retains nor maintains true femininity. Instead, it uses an imaginative lens to cultivate a masculine representation that remains ambiguous, not overwhelming the potential for fulfilling a specific masculine interaction, one that is singular and not universal. This imagination is not intended to foster a more developed femininity, but rather to stimulate a state of hibernation for femininity, available only when the right interaction arises. The imaginative masculine disposition will be enough to sustain this hibernation, status quo without demanding the development of the feminine disposition.

Masculine and Feminine Vulnerabilities

To disorder the masculine disposition is to create an environment that is not conducive to interaction. One might assume that specific hostile interactions would disrupt the masculine disposition, but in reality, the masculine's attentiveness to interaction allows it to retain its ground under duress. The same can be said for the feminine disposition: a restrictive environment is bearable because it is a habitat of regularity, enabling the supervision of environmental problems.

When an environment becomes taxing, the feminine disposition draws strength from the secluded details of that domain, finding acceptance in the realm which has been cast. The masculine disposition, however, becomes unruly under such environmental demands because it seeks interactions, but these are prescribed as the only interactions available. Instead of engaging in a structured manner which it is designed for, the masculine disposition finds itself at the mercy of a limiting sequence, which constantly reminds it of what is lost in this confined expanse, and, more importantly, of what interactions could have been possible were it not for this environmental restriction.

The feminine disposition experiences a similar loss in restrictive social interactions, which demand precision and specificity in all details. When removed from its realm of interest, the feminine disposition, which resides in the environment itself, finds these interactions taxing. The emphasis on specific masculine interactions removes the possibility of viewing masculinity from a broader, more universal perspective. The notion of direct masculine interaction is already alien to the feminine disposition, as each interaction erases the idea of the environment, rendering it environment-less. This mirrors the masculine preoccupation with specific interactions, where a restricted environment compresses its attention to the details which make up its framework. This disables its ability to interact directly, reducing it to a product of a specific environment.

Masculine and Feminine Vulnerabilities

The interaction does not require animation to meet masculine criteria. Instead, its qualities lie in specificity, which promises more than it delivers. Specificity alone does not provide adequate interaction for a developed masculine disposition because it does not lead to other possibilities and risks stagnation over time.

The purpose of interaction is to act as a conduit for a steady stream of further engagements. However, the disposition is unwilling to attend to this steady stream, instead opting for the narrow engagement that promises immediate results. There is no certainty that the steady stream will be pursued; thus, specificity becomes a balancing act for masculinity, engaging with something that is inherently another thing, yet never moving beyond the medium that leads to it.

Too much focus on the stream could lead to emasculation, as the entire environment would become the sole occupation. On the other hand, a deficiency of attention to specificity causes the disposition to disengage from reality. There are two ways the disposition can retreat from reality: it can either find specificity, which promises little to no further stream of interactions, or neglect engagement with any specificity, justifying it as overly containing or disingenuous.

When specificity becomes so narrow that no other interactions are possible, the ability to continue engaging becomes lost, leading to a form of emasculation. A failure to engage with the feminine side of interactions, or a rejection of it, will lead to a loss of a crucial aspect of masculinity: participation in feminine interactions.

When considering the two, animation is seen in quite different perspectives by each disposition. Masculinity perceives animation as a potent reservoir of further interactions, which automatically provokes a spirit of animation that delivers nuanced and continuous engagements. On the other hand, femininity sees animation as proof of feminine awareness, despite the demonstrable lack of animation that would endow the masculine disposition. Femininity will not seek animation from the masculine disposition, as it would only confirm that the masculine disposition already possesses a database of interactions, thereby negating the need for specificity.

It is precisely the absence of interactive material that leads the masculine disposition to seek out a feminine counterpart. Moreover, it is the unwillingness to settle for all interactions, where no specific feminine counterpart is necessary, which further compounds the issue. Animation is not a promising act of the masculine disposition, as commonly assumed, but rather a side feature of its abilities. The animated nature alerts the feminine disposition to the conscious endeavor of vulnerability that lies within the masculine disposition. This vulnerability, an inherent need for interactive elements, will not be fully sought out but remains an important aspect of its structure. Without animation, the masculine disposition will have no need for the interactive promise and will not utilize the feminine disposition in its intended way.

This mirrors the feminine request for the masculine disposition to display a certain feminine aspect. This request is not meant to extract a deeper understanding of femininity but to sharpen the sense of what the feminine experience is like, even as the masculine disposition remains aloof from the feminine one. Similarly, the masculine disposition may request a feminine counterpart to demonstrate a masculine trait, providing insight into what is counterintuitive to their own structure. A highly developed masculine or feminine disposition will not require many such requests, as they will naturally understand their own structure and accept the opposing side as a counterpart.

A developed feminine disposition can remain steadfast in the face of masculinity, even if such masculinity is an unfamiliar realm. The notion of innocence can be associated with both masculinity and femininity, as it is the disposition itself that leads to the dynamic without fear of failure. There is no clear pathway for the feminine-masculine dynamic, because whatever has been developed thus far is based on the disposition alone, without real-life scenarios to invoke staleness or corruption. Any corruption within the disposition, particularly innocence, cannot be attributed to the counterpart but to ignorance.

Innocence, as the organic manifestation of the masculine-feminine dynamic, presupposes the natural state of affairs. While overt attachments to these dispositions may be constructs of social development, their essence is simple and aligns with the realm of attention; the perception of the environment or specific interactions, which are the only choices for organic attention to be directed.

The relationship between the masculine and feminine dispositions also serves an organic function. Masculinity is reluctant to engage with the entirety of all information because its focus is on singular interactions. This obedience to specific interactions is a preference of the attention sphere, which chooses connotations contained by direct engagements that offer a limited amount of information without being overwhelmed by too much data; the overwhelming nature of all data.

Preference can be likened to how one's attention is drawn to a particular color. This attraction might trigger a network of thoughts, but it ultimately loops back to itself, since color preference is also biological; both biologically and locally determined. The color that resonates with the organism may lie outside conventional context, making any conceptual analysis feel like chasing one's tail. The same applies to the masculine preference for interaction. This may be explained through conceptual justification, such as masculinity being characterized by a heightened animation of detail when interaction is the sole focus. It may also be rooted in biological tendencies, where the organism favors specificity because it aligns with its biological structure.

The relationship between the two is born from necessity and vulnerability and not the direct manifestation of the disposition. In reality, the masculine disposition finds interest in the feminine disposition only after recognizing that it cannot self-provide a utility were it to remain in the masculine position. The same applies to the feminine; for itself, it does not seek the relationship and only after sensing the loss of being overwhelmed with the totality of information without a defining characteristic to offer a solid reference point. Without the ability to disrupt this overwhelming nature, the feminine turns to those who maintain that characteristic.

For both dispositions, a choice can be made: rather than enshrouding their vulnerability with a counterpart, to fulfill the vulnerability by switching sides. Since it is impossible to be both at the same time, because an organic system either perceives the environment or specific interactions, this would be a thorough switch, with a new vulnerability which still needs to be fulfilled. We must remind ourselves that this process can occur in a moment's lapse, for one instance being masculine and the other feminine, yet the vulnerability at each interval cannot be fulfilled contained by the disposition itself. The switch will not eliminate the vulnerability, as it will merely embody the full nature of that vulnerability, thereby creating a corresponding vulnerability in its counterpart. There is no instance in which one can do both, because the attention sphere functions organically to allow focus on only one point of sight at any given moment.

Thus, the relationship is a manifestation of fulfilling each other's vulnerability, but also through the acceptance of each position in their adherence to their disposition. Immediately upon the relation between masculine and feminine, each side will need to address their arguments for remaining in their disposition. Because they are open to embracing their vulnerability, the system is compelled to ask whether that vulnerability can be fulfilled without a counterpart, despite the difficulty, and in doing so, perhaps result in less shame. The relationship is a remark on the inefficiency of the disposition, leading to either having one disembark from it or retrieving supplementary justifications to remain as they were.

The argument to remain in a disposition can be perplexing because it is deeply rooted in various psychic and organic areas. The influences for masculinity can be about certain universal themes, such as self-appointing to be available to perceive things as they were; to arise at a moment's notice. This is done for the greater good of the communal system, since the personal realm would not necessarily benefit from such keenness, as it would place the organic system at the forefront of the communal system. There is also the connotation of self-sacrifice; being at the behest of the momentary observation against the backdrop of a more expansive system. The masculine disposition is already a form of self-sacrifice, as it follows a narrow attention sphere. Whatever enters that limited focus is assumed to represent the whole picture, and if it carries any hostility, it is perceived as an organic threat. We cannot argue the case of masculinity in its self-propagation and can only understand it as being appointed for a role surrounded by a communal body.

Therefore, in locales or eras of peace and prosperity, the masculine disposition does not have this motive for remaining in its field of cognition, and a more developed undertaking will be necessary to remain as they were. Society will commend the feminine disposition when one need not be available at a moment's notice, and this is also for the personal realm. If one's experiences have taught the necessity of remaining focused on the threatening nature of others, the masculine disposition will be more accessible, and the feminine will be more difficult to justify.

The alternative also true: if experiences have taught the individual that there is no need to specify themselves at any interval, they will endure a feminine disposition more easily, with the justification to be narrow, and a masculine disposition will be difficult to find. Another reason why societies that experience peace and prosperity tend to upend the process is because it motivates a stark leaning toward the feminine disposition which, in its extreme, will both lose any specificity or definition and lack self-consciousness regarding the vulnerability of not having that.

This will not only cause a leaning toward the feminine disposition but also incentivize discounting the masculine relationship as trivial and unnecessary for an unknown or archaic vulnerability. With all of this in place, vulnerability will deepen twofold, rendering society easily swayed or defeated without resistance.

Another point of the matter is that there will be a degradation of the individual, for a feminine disposition that follows its extreme, differing from the hostile nature of a masculine figure, will lose its coherence due to the information flow overriding sensibility and even the attention sphere will lose definition to be unable to distinguish information.

This happens to be another reason that incentivizes orientating toward the masculine disposition, as even in its extreme it will not lose coherence, only becoming hostile for the social environment. It can always be reversed, whereas the feminine disposition may lead to such incoherence that the pathway back to coherence is nearly impossible. Thus, we have an inclination of disrupting peace and prosperity, on both the individual and societal levels: first with the defeat of the masculine disposition and its ensuing incomprehension of the feminine's vulnerability, and then the incoherence of society or the simple takeover by any external entity.

The masculine disposition will be the cause of immense stagnation, either on the personal or societal level, because it does not decline or recess into incoherence, only becoming overly focused on an arbitrary detail that causes it to be lost to the rest of reality. The stagnation can perpetually continue because there is an element of detail that remains coherent and can produce a system of sociality.

The masculine disposition, by assuming that their attention sphere is the only probable reality, will neglect its intrinsic vulnerability: the overwhelming interactions and environments which are available. While they may recognize the presence of something beyond, they will reduce it to just another interpretation of the same reality they already perceive. In a philosophical perspective, they are correct; the narrow framework does provide a lens upon reality to which any other information will be other vantage points of that same reality. This is much like viewing a capsule and mistaking it for the entirety of the reality it signifies, despite the common understanding that a capsule is but a symbolic container, not to be conflated with the domain it reflects.

Another reason for stagnation is the swiftness with which a masculine disposition can cast off ensuing feminine aspects. Because femininity does not define itself, nor place itself in a specific orientation, the masculine disposition can simply place its minor domain of specificity to delineate the presence of undefined information. Definition will always rule out what cannot or will not be defined, only because it is a habitat of authenticity to which femininity cannot propose with certainty.

However, a developed form of femininity will be dissuaded from its position in face of masculine stagnation, yet will seep into the entire framework of the communal forum. Since it retains an array of environmental realities, by being adjacent to a masculine disposition, it will follow its course into the specific domain that is being attended by that masculinity.

The vulnerability of masculinity is the lack of awareness to the source of their informational tendencies because they only know what is before them. By simply placing new information around the masculine disposition, it will have no way of filtering that information from any other information, for they concern themselves only with the capsule of definition, not with what gives rise to it. The masculine disposition does not soberly have the capability to control the information flow which eventually leads to their attention sphere. When the masculine disposition senses that a more developed formation is being sent into their attention sphere, they have two possible choices:

Either they can accept the new information without attending to its source, in other words, remain steadfast in the position as a masculine disposition; to which it does not matter the source but only the attention to that specificity. The other choice is to not accept the stark appearance of a vulnerability into which they cannot control the entire framework they attend with such diligence. What is being proposed is that all of their masculine positions are under the rubric of a feminine source, to which they appear as subordinates, carrying out the detailed work for a source that is not meant for their hands. Although this was always the truth of the masculine disposition, having neglected this obvious vulnerability to then have it resurface can cause a disruption of the masculine disposition.

Instead of accepting that vulnerability, the masculine disposition attends to it thoroughly, following the source and all the possible material that leads to their specificity. They may begin this journey only to realize that they are beginning to take up the feminine disposition, yet are unwilling to return to the subordinate chambers and continue the work; to be ignorant of the perpetrating machines. This leads them to a stalemate, which can cause the worst activity in both personal and societal realms.

They will attempt to take control of the feminine source, as if it were a singular position of authority, and thus be able to return without the sense of that vulnerability. However, multiple problems become apparent: first, the feminine disposition is not singular but only the exposed reality that has been pursued by individuals. It cannot be dispelled, just as a new perspective cannot be "de-perspective-fied," and it is a conflict against one's psyche.

Second, the vulnerability is already exposed and cannot be undone, so the idea of forcing the source to return to its original state is a fantasy because even within their private domain, they must still contend with the persistent awareness of that vulnerability. Because of the impossibility of their pursuit, they will continue attempting to embellish or destroy habitats, an already exposed reality, but they do this at the expense of the social environment. Femininity does not go away, only becoming exposed in an even more grand manner, and the masculine disposition will not be willing to either become the feminine disposition or retreat to pre-exposed times. The obvious answer to this problem is the advent of the relationship, which serves this very purpose.

Another argument for masculinity, especially in the personal realm, is the attention to detail that serves that disposition. Contrary to appearances, when the masculine disposition is ruminating in an interactive experience, the details of that interaction are highlighted to a degree unavailable to the feminine disposition. This is why an obsessive trait can manifest with the masculine disposition, as the awareness and keenness of certain details become so vitalized that one is unwilling to disengage. Although obsession can also arise from the masculine determinant nature of attending to a specificity even as it proves to lack stimulation or reciprocity. The obsession can also arise due to the potency of experiencing information at such depth that there is a romantic sentiment as to its dynamism, which of course can lead to a more general obsession of remaining in that specific domain for an overextended period.

Masculinity/Femininity and Fear

Masculinity is afraid of the loss of its independence, not for its detachment from the source, nor for its own degeneration. These are already accepted at the onset of that negotiation; to be masculine is to enter into a realm of independence from direct reality, and even from independence of themselves. We may ask, what is independence if not the expression of selfhood?

This is answered when we realize that, in order to gain the appearance of genuine independence, masculinity is required to dismember itself from its real selfhood and build a fabricated version that does not teach itself of its connection to reality and nature. Thus, they are independent only within a fabricated version of themselves and, by that extension, of reality. They have entered into that masculine communion.

Therefore, the notion of fear, which is an expression of dread, is only found in the threat to its premise as a fabricated system. There is a deep connection to nature, suggesting that something exists independently of their bodily separations. This is not noticed by their fabricated version and, if anything, is the most repressed element. They cannot allow a clear indication of that connection, for doing so would require admitting their corporal separation and its attachment, which they cannot do.

This is where femininity ensures fairness, in that it restores the repressed and true nature of the individual by reminding the masculine disposition of their attachment to reality, even within their adhered disposition. This is also why masculinity opposes femininity so strongly: femininity presents the opportunity for that dread, threatening to disenfranchise the notion of masculinity and its stature.

With a simple reminder, femininity can open a portal that is enchanting, but just as easily, that portal can upend the entire structure, revealing the nature of reality as it truly is. Therefore, the feminine is equal in dread to masculinity as any other fear, as it represents the possibility of the system's disenfranchisement. It is not the adherence to masculinity that is so paramount, but the no-man's-land of losing that system. One cannot simply slip into the feminine side; first, one must endure an area of existential dread before that possibility.

On the other hand, fear or dread of the feminine disposition is not linked to the loss of femininity itself, but rather with the loss of the source of vitality. For in reality, everything is attached within its hierarchy of systems, so the loss of a source is not merely a loss of femininity; it is an existential confinement to utter oblivion. Of course, there is the possibility of creating a temporary masculine-type construct, in which one would be safe in their loss of the source, as it does not require a source and instead relies on itself. However, this may not be forthcoming for the feminine disposition, as entering into masculine confinement would still entail dread until that entity can be created. They also dread strong forms of masculinity, which can disrupt their connection to the source of vitality, all without the ability to recreate the masculine form; especially not at that extreme level that has been pronounced.

The masculine disposition can learn to format itself to take part in feminine ideals, so that the dread is not long-lasting, and it can quickly pivot to the feminine form and its source of vitality. The same can be said for femininity, which can learn to pivot when a source is lost, creating a masculine formation or a contrasted reality of independence where a source is neither needed nor recommended.

The Intersection of Gender Infrastructure and Violent Expression

In a theoretical model of violence rooted in gender infrastructure, violence, specifically domestic violence (and not warfare or systemic advancements), can arise from a misalignment between the structural integration of femininity as it would existentially stand and the actual, authentic feminine presence of individuals or groups. Systemic advance can be categorized by anything that is, but not limited to, the requirements of groups or systems that cannot be reduced to individual expression or group expression. Rather, it involves controlled and regulated needs, such as judicial oversight.

What is to be existential infrastructure is whatever is defined as infrastructure that reveals its relevance to the social sphere. For illustration, most developed countries have some sort of rail system, both local and intercity, although not all of these systems are the manifestation of the populace they serve. They may be placed upon the infrastructure without consideration or coordination of all the dynamic aspects they interfere with, e.g., each station's relation to private localities or destinations that are not universally regarded as ultimate by consensus. The question of creating the existential component of infrastructure is another discussion, but as long as there is agreement on its categorization, the discussion remains valid.

The existential state of infrastructure, if reduced from its initial proposition and framed as a more nuanced form of gendered femininity, will ultimately perform the opposite effect. Gender, as a rigid, prescriptive model, leads to violence not only as a tool of enforcement against those who deviate from imposed norms, but also as a reflection of the system's inability to integrate a valued, authentic feminine expression within its framework.

The Intersection of Gender Infrastructure and Violent Expression

The aggressive behaviors labeled as toxic masculinity can be seen as compensatory responses. When feminine expression is systematically denied or devalued, the resulting imbalance manifests as a failure at the systemic level. This failure legitimizes violence as a way to correct or punish deviation from the narrow gender norms imposed by the infrastructure.

In this context, two forms of violent expression can interfere with femininity: when the feminine aspect of infrastructure is repressed or undervalued by societal processes, what remains is a diminished version of femininity. This absence or misrepresentation often triggers a compensatory reaction in interpersonal dynamics.

The Biological and Psychological Foundations of Femininity

Femininity derives from two sources that are at odds with each other, existing in contrast. The first is the natural predisposition of femininity, where one is inclined, through biological development and genealogy, to direct one's psyche in a manner defined as feminine. Many elements contribute to this effect, though they share one thing in common: they originate from a biological system. There is a lineage component, such that if a parental figure has developed a system of femininity, it will biologically endure in the next generation.

When describing femininity, we must be careful, as we are already presuming the advent of mating and the scientific research surrounding evolutionary process. It is logical that nature takes precedence, since cell reproduction is the core tenet. Thus, mating and reproduction serve as the onset of feminine characteristics. We arrive at the presumption that femininity is a characteristic grounded in this long history of mating, allowing us to derive conclusions separate from the specific mating process itself and instead on the character of femininity. If a parental figure has developed this character, it will transmit to the next generation as a psychological encapsulation of femininity. This transmission is not based on the parental figure's mating strategies, but rather on the character itself, which has a predisposition shaped by mating history. As Buss explores, various mating constraints and the selection processes that establish historical precedence in the dynamics between males and females are grounded in this mating history. (Buss, 2019)[6]

This is not a composite picture of femininity, but rather the constraints and environmental factors that support healthy long-term reproduction. The character of femininity still exists, not solely based on mating history, though connected, but more so as a strategy for engaging with reality and the psychological systems underlying affection.

The Biological and Psychological Foundations of Femininity

Even if a biological element influences the attention span of female heredity across species, a psychological experience remains, not based on mating per se, but in how one interacts with all of reality. For example, a female's preference for commitment, like the female weaverbird who selects the best nest as a prerequisite for mating, involves an understanding long-term commitment. This can be viewed as the female's preference for commitment in mating, nonetheless as the weaverbird's interaction with reality and the function of a constructed nest. Furthermore, this aspect of femininity extends beyond mating, becoming a fundamental approach of nature as it differentiates between nesting and non-nesting environments. (Collias , 1973)[7]

When discussing femininity as a character, we refer to a manner of interacting with reality which traces back to mating strategies but remains distinct from them. It is an approach to reality itself, like distinguishing between nesting qualities and the broader reality set against non-nesting qualities.

To further this premise, the lineage of parental figures can imbue a character trait through the lens of differentiating nesting from non-nesting. This is not based on taught mating strategies but on biologically transferred knowledge and understanding. The child, male or female, already possesses a predisposition toward this trait. While it can be used for mating strategies, such as a female selecting a reliable male, it is not limited to that. It extends to recognizing reliability across social structures and throughout nature.

This is what we term femininity, biologically transferred through generations. It should not be confused with biological development as the sole source of continuation. While biological constraints influence masculinity and femininity, they are not the same as the character traits themselves unless one views mating not only as reproduction but as an interaction with all psychological elements within the psyche.

Thus, a child may be predisposed to a strong character formation defined as femininity. This predisposition is not shaped primarily by cultural circumstances, or at least not by current cultural systems, but by the evolution of their lineage in response to femininity. Again, it is not based on successful mating strategies across generations but on an accumulated course toward this character formation. We might even suggest that a specific ethnic group may be predisposed to femininity, not necessarily due to mating success across generations, but through inherited feminine disposition via biological transfer and intuitive learning.[8]

To extend this premise, intuitive learning and biological transfer are usually associated with feminine and masculine traits which resemble mating strategies. This is the essential requirement for lineage perpetuation through the transmission of learned experiences. Without the potential for improved mating abilities and healthier reproduction, there would be no reason to transfer such traits to the next generation.

All learning operates under the guise of mating possibility. We can view Freud's theory (1905) in an unintended manner; knowledge is vitalized by the psyche as sublimation: a sexual or mating premise is subdued to allow for an educational pattern.[9],[10]

We will reverse the premise: all learning must be vitalized by a sexual element or mating possibility, not sublimation per se, but as the coercion of a sexual element redirected toward learning. The biological system would not engage for any other reason. Both perspectives utilize the mating element, one as a promise of more perfected, delayed procreation, and the other in its natural manifestation.

The Generation, Preservation, and Evolution of Femininity

When we discuss generation, preservation, and evolution of the character of femininity, it is the usage of the mating element or the evolutionary necessity of procreation, distilled into its psychological version. One is retrieving the intuitive data of mating experience, like in how nests represent a commitment value, but instead of its utility for direct intercourse and procreation, it becomes the general view of commitment and reliability. This trait is extracted and applied as a system of ideas that are performative and aimed at the betterment of existence.

When the parental lineage follows a psychological reality where reliability is sought in all mental developments, they become predisposed to the trait of femininity, which is then taught to the generation which succeeds them. Because the mating element still remains, one can technically utilize the commitment value at any point for the outcome of better procreation; it will be a biological consideration transmitted through one's genes.

However, unless we find an outcome where that very commitment value incurs a cost to procreation itself, such as when one stifles the female from autonomous function, thereby disrupting the utility of that feminine trait overall, the premise of directing the psyche toward reliability will remain intact. If this adverse effect on mating elements arises, then adherence to the continuing trait would result in extreme masculinity or, when engaged by the psyche as a means of attenuating reality; a decline of true femininity.

We can imagine this dynamic playing out: a female seeking reliability might reach an outcome that proves dissatisfactory, leading her to abandon that trait. The male may either assume nothing has changed or lose the ability to respond to any real-time expression of femininity, thereby becoming purely masculine. Meanwhile, the female who still values such a trait is also disrupted in her expression of femininity, directly linked to mating benefits, continuing her pursuit based on a past that is now bygone. In this scenario, the trait of reliability would no longer be considered part of the genuine masculine-feminine dynamic until it is validated in the mating arena.

When a parental figure transfers femininity, they are not offering a trait per se but rather the contextual overlay of the full form of femininity. This constitutes the formation of how mating maps out, despite the particular directions it could take, and represents a universal femininity that cannot change unless an evolution or biohacking of a great magnitude occurs.

For example, take the trait of the weaverbird, nesting; a specific direction within universal femininity. To what is nesting owed? The continuation of parental care. To what is that owed? Better offspring. And what is the benefit of better offspring? The continuation of evolutionary demands. Why does the female seek this out more than the male? She seeks better evolution, whereas the male does not. Why is that so? She is following nature's system, whereas he is antagonistic to it. How could he disobey his nature? Because there is a female to take up the task, allowing individuality to be engaged despite nature's demands.

Why must each take specific roles? The rule of nature is that one can only be either of two things: nature's expression or individuality against nature's demand. These two forces are embodied in the male and female for the final outcome of a perfected form. This would be what constitutes universal femininity in this context: the representation of nature as it is, and as it will be, according to its current system. With this in mind, the trait of reliability is something that nature may seek out at intervals to sustain what is current, but it is not universal. Unreliability and spontaneity are paramount to nature and can either be a trait of masculinity or femininity, depending on the mating outcome.

In an environment where deviation is required, it is the masculine disposition that provides this to the female. In an environment where stability is more beneficial, then such becomes the trait of masculinity. The female, in this context, is neither stable nor unstable but rather a representation of nature, where both those traits are required at intervals. Surely, we may have an inclination to say that the female disposition is mostly stable and the masculine unstable, but that is determined by environmental requirements.

It would seem that since the male is meant to be independent of nature, unreliability is his natural habitat. However, independence and unreliability do not go hand in hand. This is where confusion can arise, where unreliability is assumed to be independence, granting the male justification to persist in that regard despite the feminine mating requirement of the moment.

The opposite is also true; we never reach a place where the masculine disposition should become completely dependent, as that would contradict the male's role as an individual *of* nature and lead him into the realm of universal femininity. However, and this is a strong clause, reliability may be a necessary trait, as it is based not on dependence but on a form of independence that is firm in its movements.

Femininity, Vitality, and the Perception of Nature

The female, in retracting her step to become a fully embodied exemplar of nature, or more precisely, in aligning with everything nature-related, follows the source of vitality as a universal characteristic of femininity. Vitality, in this context, is the sensibility of reaching a more pronounced experience of one's inherent system: the source of oneself. It is the realization of the experience of *experience* itself, which is the closest one can come to being a fabric of nature.

The reason this realization is more prominent than simply being, which could be claimed as the most inherent aspect of nature, is that femininity requires a form of masculinity. Yes, to be sure, *being* itself is the furthest arena of femininity, but it does not account for the independence of individuality that masculinity espouses.

In such a proposition, femininity without that partialization of masculinity would be like a tree existing without anyone perceiving it, not like a tree or a bush in an eloquent poem that is reflected upon. We could even say that extreme femininity, like the tree itself, is primed to be at the juncture of extreme masculinity. A tree, without our mention of it, is independent of nature. Nature, by definition, is not inherent but rather a perception, "nature" as we see it. A tree does not inherently seem attached to other elements of nature; it is only our proposition of nature that integrates it into a fuller system. Nature is based on our perception of it, which then makes it a case for femininity.

The same can be said for masculinity: when brought to the extreme, where independence exists without dependence and individuality is truly individual, it ventures into the formation of femininity in its extreme. For when one must espouse individuality with such veracity, they are, in truth, building the assurance that they are most needful of their nature as a dependent part of a system.

Femininity, Vitality, and the Perception of Nature

The source of vitality cannot be found through independence, for individuality is secluded from systems and external elements, and vitality is not inherent to a single organism. The source is also not found within the individual system, because the individual is not self-contained but rather a product of their surrounding environment.

Take an economic example: an individual does not contain currency of value unless they are connected to a system beyond themselves. Even raw materials such as food and water are not contained within the individual; they require availability, procurement, and digestion. This necessitates freedom, both politically and structurally, and even more so, the procurement of such material items depends on a geographical amenity, one that is often contested or occupied by political groups. If not them, the animal kingdom itself would be surveying that amenity. Whatever we postulate, the source is always derived from outside the individual: in birth, from parents, and in death, from the earth.

Thus, the recurring notion of autonomy as an ideal—what Fineman (2004) highlights as the lack of transparency between political categories in their use of dependency and independence, assumes that the source of vitality is found within the opening of the individual if only one dug deep enough. In fact, we find the opposite to be true. The fewer free markets there are, where individuals and groups retain currency value, the less wealth is procured. There is a drastic loss of value when economic pockets remain independent, while significant development occurs when systems interact.[11]

Thus, the source of vitality for the expression of one's natural state of being is found through its reflection in accordance with the systems it is attached to and dependent upon. The feminine character can be seen as the driving force in maintaining attachment and proximity to its source of vitality, which, ironically, is not truly theirs but rather a function of their embeddedness in the surrounding environment. In accordance with this, we see that the masculine disposition contradicts this premise, or at least provides the dynamic inference that *being* itself is complementary to itself. While this may be less true as an overarching premise, it remains paramount in the organic development of the individual, where personal parameters are recognized.

There is a dissociation from the source of vitality, where vitality is not the ideal but rather functionality; which only becomes functional when there is a feminine opposition proclaiming a universal nature that then undermines the grasp of individuality. When the feminine disposition does not align with this idea, the masculine disposition cannot claim a functionality of independence, for that would already be the feminine experience. Instead, it would fall upon the masculine disposition to remind femininity of its own nature, to extract being itself and place it before them.

This, in itself, is an act of femininity: tending to nature in order to retell its story. But it is also a notion of functionality, as one acknowledges that a *thing* itself cannot see itself. Of course, the feminine disposition can retract from the embodiment of being in order to reflect upon itself, but this then enters masculine territory, where individuality is defined by its parameters despite being embedded within systems. It is then upon the masculine disposition to provide a stronger argument for individuality, to proclaim an independence so stark that it compels the feminine realm to recognize its need not to be like, or even to be contrary to that independence, for it appears distasteful and untrue at a fundamental level.

Alternatively, the masculine disposition may take the opposite route, entering into the feminine state to dispel the makeshift independence that is being arranged. Through this approach, masculinity extracts a more nuanced understanding, making the feminine disposition realize the nature of its *being* rather than merely proclaiming its parameters.

Context vs. Interactivity

The dispositions of femininity and masculinity are based on a contextual formula rather than an interactive formula. The masculine disposition generates a sort of contextual perception of reality, in which the interactive base of that context is of little consequence, and only the contextual outflow matters. In this way, we might assume that the masculine disposition is also the one that actualizes structural reality, because it is the case that the contextual attention is the culmination of interactivity, which is also the cusp of the actualized process.

What is most interactive is least available to be actualized. It does not work the other way around; what is most contextualized is not necessarily most actualized, because it is possible that contextual frameworks extend beyond actualization. However, we could state the clause that an actualization is devoid of nuanced interactivity.

This, as we said, is an assumption, and we might even say, it is a rather wrong assumption, because the contextual perspective, which happens to parallel with actualization, does not necessarily coincide. More likely, interactive dispositions are more permeable to an actualized system, while contextualized formulas are disruptive.

For example, technological systems include the notion that interactivity is of more importance than the contextual overlay. Yet, simple construction will always be formulated from a stronger contextual basis, while the architectural realm and its variable activities form the basis of a progressive system. Therefore, actualization is not parallel to contextual layers, and depending on the society and social environment, it may either afford interactivity or a contextual perspective.

We could say that the basis of all interactions is *interactivity*, and the contextual overlay serves to formulate and extrapolate that very interactivity. Thus, we have many who take feminine experience and extrapolate such to a level that it loses its feminine undertone and instead takes a more masculine shape.

Context vs. Interactivity

This may lead us to assume that the feminine disposition is the perfect form, and the masculine disposition is the overlay. This is a correct assumption insofar as a feminine disposition that does not comprise a contextual extrapolation of its substance, one which begins to overwhelm its innate system. If there is a focal point of the interactive experience, then it could be the case that the feminine disposition favors one aspect over another, or the majority over the minority, or any process where there is a lack of amelioration among all interactivity. What results is an unstable experience of interactivity, with interactive pockets that neither communicate with each other nor allow the feminine disposition to initiate forward-looking progress.

There are two methods to prevent the feminine disposition from confining to an interactive experience missing continuity. The first method is to contextualize and disseminate the interactive experience as a masculine disposition would perform; extending to an understanding of microscopic proportions. This method requires a masculine attribute that allows for the interactivity process to take place, as well as the ability to detach from interactivity to formulate specific aspects, thereby adding to masculine attributes.

The feminine disposition, which does not require this masculine attribute, deals with interactivity and its cyclical spiral through a method of ameliorating all interactivity. This method is as follows: all interactivity should be in constant availability for amelioration, and prior interactive states should be recognized as superior and permeable for as long as they last. Instead of extending the interactive aspect itself (a masculine attribute), this allows the interactive vitality to permeate all its compartments.

When we find the feminine disposition allowing for heightened emotional availability for interactive substance, some are based on the principle of improving all forms of interactivity. This is only possible through a sensitive understanding of interactive states and their potential for improvement. For example, the feminine tendency to cry is not merely a biological response but a philosophy aimed at ameliorating the current emotional state, which would not be possible without a deep, introspective mending that manifests with tears.

The masculine disposition, on the other hand, does not concern itself with overexposure or a lack of interactivity. Instead, it follows whatever interactive basis is available at the moment, moving into a contextual sphere. If there is a shortage of interactivity, it will extrapolate from whatever prior interactions exist, so the final product becomes highly contextualized based on the available memory of interactivity. The closer we reach to interactivity itself, the less we need to rely on contextual background for meaning. The interactivity is competent enough within the individual that stretching its details further becomes a simple task. As interactivity permeates the psyche and occupies its availability, whatever remains requires more focused contextual deliberation to sustain viability.

This explains why anxiety may arise from a lack of interactivity, because any attempt to stretch the context is based on relatively undeveloped states of interactivity. Furthermore, extrapolating from these already permeated states may lead to details that no longer match the current interactive needs.

The continuous contextual elaboration may be a natural manifestation of the masculine disposition. However, if it isn't offered an interactive aspect that hasn't been integrated into the system, it may instead retrieve from prior interactive states, which can disrupt the balance. When an interactive experience has already permeated the psyche, it is no longer viable unless extrapolated for further details. However, this will also create a reality framework that validates experiences which the psyche hasn't endured in such a way.

This is the case for a masculine disposition facing a dearth of interactivity. Yet there is an alternative: the masculine disposition may experience overexposure to multiple vantage points of interactivity, which primes it to extrapolate from relevant material. The same challenge arises, though, in a different form: with multiple unintegrated aspects of interactivity, if the masculine disposition takes context from one specific interaction, it will do so at the expense of another. As a result, the masculine disposition may need to borrow from the feminine disposition's method of amelioration, as it cannot provide direction for every interactive demand, making some experiences permeable at the cost of others. For instance, if it follows the most recent, low-profile interactive experience along a contextual line of thought, it may sacrifice a prior high-profile interaction, disrupting the overall contextual structure. Instead of simply stretching interactivity, it halts other interactive processes, creating an anxious environment.

Masculinity, Femininity, and the Infrastructure of Identity

Masculinity represents existential infrastructure, not the appeared or proclaimed version, but its true element, foreclosing its real sense of femininity. For this very reason, masculinity becomes deeply invested in the actualization of the human embodiment of femininity, for it may claim a certain feminine assertion that is not aligned with the infrastructural version. It is not that masculinity is disturbed by a simple representation that goes awry, but rather that humankind is found to be faulty in that it proposes a deep misalignment between the femininity espoused by individuals and the infrastructure to which all must ultimately conform as the final touch of proper actualization.

The truth of the matter, where the individual is concerned, is this: why can't one propose a liminal version of femininity without concern for where the infrastructural setting is contained? When femininity is understood not as an individual trait, but as a communal proposition, then we must contend with its integration throughout the system.

Moreover, masculinity will enjoin itself as an exemplified femininity not for its distinct case, but for its ability to grant access to a more complete and wholesome scope of consciousness.

Femininity, Infrastructure, and Representation

There is a strange problem that arises when femininity intersects with infrastructure, particularly in its representation. Since femininity is, in some sense, the pronounced exuberance of sexuality, whereas masculinity may or may not be, it follows that femininity must recognize its position in relation to infrastructure and representation. Representation, in turn, affects the extent to which that sexual exuberance is expressed or validated within the representational system.

For example, or rather, for illustration, if the infrastructure is lacking, and yet sexual exuberance continues, then it will be perceived by the infrastructure not as a representation (for it doesn't comprise that level of competency), but rather as a highly interactive system of sexuality. The final result is a perceived notion that this representation is not part of a system, but rather is the center of that system, much like how a train station residing in lower infrastructure becomes the center of that realm. Not because it represents a continuance surrounded by the whole infrastructure, but rather despite it, as a mechanism of entering and exiting toward a destination of higher representation. Femininity will endure the same effect, in that it will be perceived by the infrastructure as the center of its entire representation, because there is no better or more complete representation to provide continuance.

The same aspect finds itself on the other side, in which femininity has an exuberance of sexuality in regard to a specific interactive aspect that does not provide a wholesome representation. In alignment with infrastructure, that interactivity could be in sequence, so that it does not provide any more exuberance other than what the infrastructure is already known for. In the event that the interactivity is of a lower regard than the infrastructure, then the infrastructure, or the representation it, will regard this femininity as a shadow, as is the case of any pronounced interactivity in a higher representational system.

That would be the alternative example, in which the train station is in a highly complex representational infrastructure. Instead of providing a representational effect, it does the opposite and pronounces itself as an interactivity, into which it becomes the shadow of that realm. This is another reason why, outside that infrastructure, train stations are given freedom in their representation. For that is the one thing that cannot be represented in a highly complex representational system, for the reason that it denotes a strong degree of interactivity that does not align with continued representation.

This is what we call strange, for femininity is bound to infrastructure in such a way that if its exuberant sexuality exceeds the capacity of the infrastructure, it will be perceived as the center and excessively engaged with; but if it is too minimal, it will be seen as merely a shadow. The question that arises is: can there be an alleviation from femininity where it no longer exuberates any form of sexuality, whether representational or highly interactive?

It seems that if there is an alleviation of femininity, then the alternative would be masculinity, so that femininity that dethrones said gender would automatically enter into a masculine orientation. Thus, there is no recognition of representation for either sexuality or interactivity, because both are assumed and manifested in masculine form.

The reason unity does not directly align with infrastructure is that it does not embody this sexual exemplification, but rather either interacts with it or does not. In some sense, the difference between masculinity and femininity in this context is the fact of choice regarding sexual exuberance. Masculinity has the choice, not because of some embellishment, but rather because there is a distance between itself and sexual orientation. It is as if masculinity is once-removed from sexuality so that it could either enter into the domain of sexuality or stay out of it.

The realm separate from sexuality that masculinity embodies is not a new form of gender, but rather a vantage point upon sexuality that only has a sentience because of sexuality. In the context of sexuality, there is no way to fully divorce oneself from it; rather, one can occupy a vantage point, much like suburbia in relation to the city. Suburbia does not bear the consequences of the city's existential development, yet it also lacks full awareness of the city's dynamics, just as this vantage point lacks full awareness of sexuality.

The Formation of the Superego and Feminine Complex

As we've noted in other works, the dichotomy between external forms and the internal conceptual realm can always be furthered. In accordance with this, it is possible that supplementary forms of infrastructure take part in one's internalized state, so that we must understand its conceptual form and correspondingly its relationship to the preliminary phase on the external front.

Although there will always be a conceptual arrangement of the interpreted version of its external parallel, it is possible that the internalized form is not part of an elaborate network of ideas and conclusions, so that it is almost in its objective to interpret rather than to partake in a psychic representation. For example, as Freud may note, the superego is an internal recreation of the authority figure, especially the parental figure, which has been internalized. Instead of it being an external form or a dynamic relationship between the self and parental figures, it becomes the state of the psyche to activate its own persona to re-exemplify that process.

Whatever the case may be, the superego, or the reformatted conceptual outlay of an external form, is not the same construct. Moreover, it must refer to the original external form so that, in totality, it is two unique aspects which correlate. Each will need its own peculiar understanding for this to be successful. In the case of femininity, it is also of the same regard, but instead of the superego, it would be considered the *feminine complex*. The feminine complex is the rearticulated version for the psyche, which correlates with but does not exemplify external femininity.

Superego vs. Feminine Complex

Much of the time, we can solve equations in that domain, as we did in the early 20th century with the superego construct. Differing from the superego, which is particular to parental or authoritative representations, the feminine complex correlates to all forms of femininity associated with much of the external world. In this way, the problem is met more head-on because the matter in which it submerges is not due to haphazard associations, but to every moment of worldly interaction. This also seems to be the solution, for by the very nature of its onset, it does not leave enough room for neurosis. Not that it does not arise, but that, at the very least, one will build a formidable system of interaction to satisfy both the feminine complex and external femininity.

The superego does not have this advantage. For, being closely linked and associated with parental figures, it will be the case that one only needs to suffice with an active role in the environment that avoids such associations. In the case of the feminine complex, if there is an ascendancy of neurosis, it is due to a reconfiguration of both systems. Instead of external associations being the cause or remedy, it is the manner of conceptual contrast that brings about both the problem and the solution.

The superego would seem to the child as a habitable problem that can be environmentally controlled, while the feminine complex would seem to be one that can be conceptually controlled. In this way, we often do not find feminine exemplification to be the cause of distress for one's feminine complex, that is, in the case of conceptual difficulty. Although this now brings the larger difficulty that separates, once and for all, the superego from the feminine complex: its problems ascend more socially than psychologically, whereas in the case of the former, it is the opposite.

We could recognize how all of one's actions either align with or differ from their superego, just as we could do the same with the feminine complex. Yet one will avoid agreeing that all social happenstance is directly related to the superego because it is a generalization of the psyche, whereas it would be more kind to the psyche to understand most social problems as based on, or in differentiation from, the feminine complex.

The reason it would not be considered a generalization is that it resides at the seat of consciousness, orienting the feminine complex. It is not subliminal and can often be brought into social discourse without difficulty. In contrast, the superego is usually avoided in everyday conversation due to its over-generalized nature. This changes, however, when discussing parental figures, which touch on the domain of the superego. Even then, it remains a challenging issue because one does not typically engage with the seat of experience from that perspective, especially in contemporary society.

Alternatively, the social point of conjecture could center on the parental figure and the superego, particularly in nomadic or head-of-household societies, while the feminine complex and its external representation of femininity may lack social regularity. This lack of regularity could lead to the belief that femininity doesn't reside at the seat of current experience.

This perspective focuses on what constitutes regular social experience within the psyche, rather than the inborn development that has yet to play a social role, whether internally or externally. We're not addressing why a particular complex becomes part of social regularity, but rather acknowledging that it is not necessarily the feminine complex or the superego that must be discussed based on social accessibility. Instead, these elements represent the most pressing social issues, making them the most worthwhile subjects for discussion.

Origins of Complex Formation

What sets this principle apart from superego-related theses is that, historically, discussing the complex related to parental figures was once socially prevalent. In contrast, the feminine complex has become the focal point of social engagement and discussion.

While we do have a notion of how the superego complex develops, it is crucial to recognize that it is the external figure's interpretive data that first triggers the formation of the complex. Once an individual gains the ability to interpret this data, they can construct it to the point where it feels like an obligation, regardless of incoming perceptual data.

The same applies to the feminine complex: interpreting data about femininity and its masculine counterpart begins the process of building what we call the feminine complex. From the first moments of life, individuals start interpreting femininity as an experience. If there were a philosophical inquiry, it might even delve into biological stature itself.

Thus, interpreting femininity kicks off the process of constructing a coherent understanding of what femininity is, ultimately leading to the formation of the feminine complex. Similarly, the superego begins by interpreting parental figures, ultimately recognizing what it means to be a parent. The individual does not embody the parental state per se; rather, they start developing the superego complex.

Feminine Complex, Superego, and the Disciplinary Failure of Form

The embodiment of the parental figure is a social understanding of the complex, not a literal embodiment of the parental figure itself. It is a reconfiguration based on a data stream that has accumulated considerable understanding of what constitutes the parental figure.

In the same way, the feminine complex follows a similar trajectory. After an interpretive stage of what constitutes femininity, one begins to approach the subject of creating or constructing the entire feminine experience as an internal state. In this process, they start to embody femininity. However, at all times, it remains the feminine complex because it is grounded in interpretive data, and once that data is processed, indifference follows.

This is why the feminine complex is more likely to emerge in early adolescence, compared to the superego complex. The interpretive data of the superego particularly that of the parental figure, becomes more precise by the age of three or four, allowing the child to begin building a construct for the superego. However, the feminine disposition lacks an immediate, clear form of femininity. While we might consider a mother or sisters as representations of femininity, to the child, they don't embody femininity until enough interpretive data is gathered to understand femininity as a concept. The process of forming a feminine interpretation starts from uncertain ground and requires significant interpretive development, more so than the final, stable understanding of femininity itself.

Cultural Variations and Developmental Contexts

The reason for this is simple: there are contesting geometrical forms of the external forms, so that what is considered a mother is not lost as a feminine experience, and what constitutes a sister is now divergent from its namesake as a feminine figure.

The entire construct of the family body correlates to the construct that is considered the family body, so that the roles that embody the family body will play more dominantly in childhood development. At the developmental stage, it is in how one internalizes their parental figure and thereby creates the superego. Instead of viewing the mother as a feminine leader, it is rather one which constitutes the superego role or the parental authoritative semblance.

In this way, again, we begin to realize that it is foremost the result of the social seat of experience, whereas the domesticity as an understood system take precedence over the feminine and masculine constructs. So that, in a society where domestication is in the background and the family bodies are delineated, it is then possible for the feminine figure to present itself as a geometrical form for the child, because they do not retain the concepts of father and mother at an existential level, and are thus more available to the feminine construct.

This is why, in nomadic systems, where the household is not subject to simplistic forms of father, mother, sister, and brother, but rather heads-of-household and complex familial expansions, it loosens the domestic experience and the familial construct. Now, the geometrical forms for the child will approach the subject of femininity and masculinity earlier than in societies with strong domestic constructs.

Early Feminine Overload and Superego Delay

We notice this when we provide a child with a high degree of conceptual information about femininity, causing them to develop the feminine complex at a much earlier age than a child not exposed to that data. We could, in theory, provide the geometrical forms to the child at the inception, so that we could place before them all possible material that constitutes the feminine experience, so that by age five or six, they are already ascertaining the feminine   complex.

But because the child can only interpret external forms within one criterion, they will have given up on familial constructs as a mechanism of perception and therefore would not build a formidable superego within their psyche. As a result, they may never develop the superego complex that is renowned as a psychological phenomenon.

In this way, we find that difficulties with authority later in life may correlate not to a disproportionate construct of the superego, but rather to a lack of data material for interpretation, so that there is no construct of the superego to correlate with the authoritative role of the external realm. Moreover, they may struggle to apply that association to their own superego.

Instead, it seems as though the authoritative figure is domineering and prepared to overtake the entire social system of the psyche. However, the psyche is actually vulnerable to this because the superego, or parental figure, provides a necessary layer of separation between internal sociality and the regular functioning of the psyche, serving as an authoritative system that controls and regulates its processes.

Superego and the Loss of Feminine Experience

This means that the parental figure and the superego complex are necessary to correlate with a civilized structure, which importantly requires authoritative outlines for every part of its network. In this way, we find that an overridden superego, where the child is constantly receiving interpretive data to the point that the superego becomes formidable, inhibits the development of the feminine complex. This happens because the child becomes so entrenched in the superego modality and focused on interpreting the external world that they see feminine forms merely as another aspect of the superego.

The superego's primary function is that of outlining and regulating its internal system, so that when it approaches the subject of feminine form, it views it either as something to incorporate or to set an outline upon, to which one never has access to the sociality or the romantic experience of selfhood surrounded by the feminine form. However, if the superego is extremely malleable, entering the sphere of the feminine form would not constitute a breach since femininity itself is a uniquely significant aspect within the network of perceptual experience.

As noted by Freud, the superego does have a preliminary stage in which it begins its enterprise as something related to the feminine form, so that we can't say that in all constructs of the superego, there remains a feminine complex, and in all feminine complexes, there remains a superego system.[12]

The reason they are separated is that they are, in fact, separated by the parents themselves, for the parental figure is both the authoritative figure and the feminine exemplification, being both a mother and a wife (for a father) and a husband; and that very dichotomy, that of either relationship or hierarchy of authority, is a dichotomy inherent in all of nature's systems.

However, it is worth inquiring into which conflicts one is being dealt, so that if it is mostly a construct of the superego, it is worth introducing the recognition of what the superego consists of; and if it is the feminine complex, it would be more apropos to approach it from that angle in the social realm.

When one reaches the stage where the feminine complex is fully established, they begin to experience femininity as an internal state, so that any external feminine form serves merely as a reflection of that internal construct; just as the superego, in its final form, corresponds to parental figures as symbolic representations rather than continuing to develop its own structure.

They have begun the stage in which the external form is just a mechanism of recalibration, more than the experience itself, so that femininity is now not in its external embodiment but an internal form, and the superego is now not in external embodiment but rather an internal structure.

The social ramification of a fully developed feminine complex is that the actual feminine counterpart does not interact with objective masculinity, for the individual has already incorporated the feminine complex, so that they interact with the external feminine form as though from the vantage point of that internalized femininity more than the masculine stage. We could imagine the social disruption which follows such a union, to which on one side you have a feminine form with the wishful attempt at approaching themselves from femininity, only to find that instead of gaining the masculine counterpart, they gain a feminine complex which has been incorporated into the masculine system so that in some sense they are absent from real masculinity.

But in the same way, we find the feminine complex satisfied at the expense of the entire subjective system, which does not accept the feminine complex as a material experience of femininity and is at a loss for a true masculine-feminine experience. Similarly, the superego complex, at its essential stage, has become ostracized from authoritative or parental forms. This is because they have already constituted all that is needed for such an understanding. However, one does not experience regulation and alignment merely because they have developed their superego, since it is also an internalized system that follows its own whims. It does not incorporate the regulation and control of everything, but instead acts according to how it sees itself as a construct

Moreover, the rest of the psychic system does not accept the construct of the superego but merely follows it. When the superego "isn't looking," so to speak, the system begins to follow its own processes, as noted by Freud as the Id, requiring one to follow external authoritative processes, with the superego complex lacking autonomy as the regulating factor.[13] This becomes a dominion upon the rest of the social aspects of the psyche, because perceptual data has been recognized: the police officer, for example, is perceived as dominating the entire system, rather than simply serving as a mechanism of regulation.

But this only becomes possible when one becomes capable of either differentiating from the superego complex or accepting its internalized state, thereby becoming open to the more prominent external form. The hostility felt toward authoritative representations correlates to the elevation of their own superego as a construct, yet this is not accepted by the rest of the psyche. This may also indicate that one does not possess a constructed superego, so that any external domination is perceived as a total control of their entire psychic happenstance.

The intermediate stage arises when interpretive data is forthcoming, but has not yet developed into a sophisticated psychic construct, still short of engaging with the external form in a meaningful way, lacking a representational model or internal organization. This intermediary complexity, especially in the feminine complex, results in a degeneration of both the external experience of feminine form, often confused with the data, and the perceptual sphere in accordance with the internal construct. The eternal feminine complex remains unpronounced and thus disruptive, though not fully perceptible.

This can be understood as akin to the persona of a schoolboy who appreciates the external feminine form, while also finding himself confused by the feminine complex, which remains unrealized and disrupts his attachment to the external form. It is similar to understanding the geometric form of an isosceles trapezoid without recognizing the significance of its equal parallel lines, so that, when constructing the shape, it's vaguely identified but not clearly pronounced. The internal mechanism can recognize the shape, but without conformity, both realms become confused.

Not only is the schoolboy in the advance of their feminine complex, to which they are laid with disparity between the perceptual data and the internal complex, but it is also in a degeneration of the feminine complex, to which, if one loses that development as an internal construct, they begin to interact with the feminine form not so much as a pure externality, nor as a correlation of a competent internal construct.

This would be similar to the superego, which can degenerate just as much, where one loses their construct as an authoritative role in their psyche. For instance, if someone follows an Eastern tradition that opposes the superego and seeks the meditative pronouncement of all parts of experience without much structure, they may lack the ability to interact with an external parental figure as a domineering force. In contrast, an individual raised within an Eastern tradition would simply view the external authoritative figure as an unquestionable source of authority, bearing no conflict. In our case, however, if one follows this tradition without the preliminary development of a superego construct, the figure is not automatically implanted onto the psyche. Instead, it becomes decompensated and deconstructed through the degradation of the superego complex.

If one has never developed a superego complex, they will not find disparity with authority because there is no mechanism contained by the psyche to disrupt that dominion, and it is rather domination without consideration, almost as if there is an indifference to the authoritative form; the way a child simply follows the parents without consideration. It is only after a preliminary superego complex develops that the child begins the lifelong battle of corroborating with the external authoritative form, because they haven't developed the superego complex in enough stature that it can inform and correlate between itself and its external form, but instead is in this arena of disruption.

Commentary and Collapse of the Feminine Complex

Initial competency that allows for the feminine complex is now serving to disrupt the perceptual data from the femininely external form. This is because it cannot be forgotten as a construct as it sits back and almost offers commentary on the feminine form instead of having to serve as a construct to correlate with the external form. It begins the commentary because it doesn't have enough of its own virtue to seem accessible as if having a complex, but consequently must make amends with the already-streamlined data. So instead, we have this purportment of interaction with the perceptual data that constantly contrasts it with a kind of suboptimal system, almost like a critique offered by someone under-informed about the subject they're critiquing.

This can occur very naturally through the process of degeneration, where the substantiated complex is not given its due regard, which either can occur through missing external forms or from misappropriation of the data to which the construct commenced in the first place. We find this readily existing in the case of one who takes the role of authority figure, especially of a high stature, where they begin to lose the external form of what constitutes an authoritative hierarchy, so that their superego, that of internal authority, does not have a correlated form to realign and reacquaint; an establishment of degeneration transpires.

In that process, having lost the construct of the superego in a unified form, they begin to breach upon the authoritative role as a source of data to gain an entranceway into the internal form of that superego, so that they end up reaching for external authority not so much for the ability of subservience, but rather inaccessibility to the authority of experience; to inform on the superego construct to make the psyche a proper happenstance. The reason they don't become subservient to an authoritative form is because they do not have enough of a construct within the superego complex to seek out its parallel in external form. They rather find themselves unable to reach into that data stream as a form of objective research and instead enter a union of exploring power within themselves and how such an ability can then inform the superego.

One cannot competently research a phenomenon or aspect when they don't have their identifiable complex as an internal reservoir to mirror and contrast; in order to inform one side over the other. Instead, in the attempt to gain entrance into that external aspect, they begin a commentary process, which doesn't correlate to an internal complex that is underserved, and instead, one becomes available to the ways in which they interact with the external form in accordance with the entire infrastructure of the psyche, separate from the complex itself.

If one were to explore authority in its external form from within the habitat of the psyche, surely there would be a form of resentment; for nothing about the intrinsic state of the psyche would like to be regulated and controlled, as it must lose its own sense in the process. So that, in informing upon authoritative forms, one would need their internal authority form, because if not, the developmental aspects of the psyche will correlate and thus become commentary. But not only commentary, resentful commentary, due to the distrust of losing that very sociality.

The same applies to the feminine complex, where one approaches the external feminine form with a weakened construct of the feminine complex, along with the general sociality of the psyche, not only within the feminine construct but across all related experiences, so that in interacting with the external form, they draw from that sociality. The problem is that the feminine complex serves as a distinct discipline of the psyche, correlating between internal and external forms. If the entire social experience of one's psyche gains access to the feminine form, especially with the preceding data of the feminine complex assisting to some degree, they will embody the femininity without any ability to stop or restrain it.

In such a case, one becomes the feminine experience in all their existential parts; or they resent, to a strong degree, the approach of such intense femininity that it takes over their entire experience because there is no discipline to regulate the process. They will both embody the hidden elements of their true feminine state (because they've embodied it at an exceptional level), while still resenting that very experience due to the diminutive substrates that are left from the original feminine complex.

Had this scenario played itself out without one bearing the feminine complex in the first place, it wouldn't have approached such degeneration because there would be no criteria to view the feminine form in any special manner. It is comparable to one who doesn't understand the beginning stages of geometry: they will not view forms when they approach the world because they haven't been introduced to that subject yet. Once they have the preliminary data it sets the stage to disrupt the rest of the psyche.

Needless to say, once the psyche gains access to the entire feminine database, while a weakly developed feminine complex serves as the conduit for informing the feminine form, the result is that the entire psyche becomes disruptive to that form, much like how the authoritative form is disrupted for someone with a weakened superego.

Critique without Complex: The Misreading of Form

In the case of the preliminary stage, where it is both without the complex and the external form, as we've noted to be the advancing stage or a period of degeneration, the information will be informed based on the permeability of comprehensiveness and not simply the arena of the complex. This admixture would cause both functional analysis, on the part of the feminine complex or the superego, in which an understanding is based on an embodied state that is disciplined and distinct within the preambles of the psyche, and then dysfunctional analysis, more so dysfunctional because of the permeability of comprehensive data that will have the information form from the sporadicity of the perceptual data and its forms. So that, in the case of the feminine complex, it would be the feminine form, and in the case of the superego, it would be the authoritative figure.

It is critical by nature because one cannot access external forms in the comprehensive state of society, because the former is with permeability that is not disciplined or able to pinpoint specificity in form, and the latter is form that demands a coherence that is separate from the rest of nature and is treated as a unified singularity. What makes it critical is that it does not understand, and therefore from that misunderstanding it is assumed that the form itself is the problem, rather than the lack of understanding.

We can follow this exercise in any form of criticism that is not discipline-oriented, which would simply be a conscious comparison, where the critical nature is first based on a dearth of understanding which then culminates in analysis. One cannot become critical of aspects or forms that lack their corresponding disciplines unless those aspects falsely proclaim understanding, in which case their absence becomes subject to analysis. Laden within the entire analysis will be noticed the discrete aspect of how the subject is truly inaccessible to their mindset, because it is in fact inaccessible to the entire psyche, as any subject would be without its disciplined correlative complex.

Thus, to be critical is to be proclaiming oneself as misunderstanding the object, while still maintaining some coherence, or, if we're going to be true to the psychological happenstance, it would be the case that it is their own measure of willingness to gain entrance into the complex, more so than the external form that represents it. This is why the authoritative figure will be claimed with disdain for the weakened superego, as to gain entrance into that very superego complex, as if the external figure is the one who provides form for the superego, and not an internal mechanism for that construct. It is a misappropriation, because although the external form is the initial state for the superego complex, it is not the location of the provision, relying instead on the psyche's internal construction. There is disdain because of the added sentimentality of the rest of the psyche, which is now open to participation in the experience of authoritative aspects, which, for regular psycho-sociality, is naturally problematic, for it demands from the onset the subservience to such dominion.

The feminine complex doesn't include that last notion, because although there may be disdain from the loss of its internal construction, which now becomes representative within femininity, it is still not due for the stain of regular psyche sociology, because it is rather somewhat coherent for those aspects to partake in feminine expression, so that it is no long stretch to demand the entire psyche to enter into that arena. However, the entire notion of femininity is based on the complex, not on the rest of the psyche, so with its degradation, it compels the complete embodiment of femininity throughout the psyche.

PART TWO: SEXUALITY

Pleasure

Sexual Dynamics and Pleasure

In any interaction, an objective is always necessary to direct the actions of the participants. The craft of integration involves each member foreseeing a gain within their own subjective experience. Pleasure serves as the intermediary since, in partaking in such a dynamic, each party seeks to experience that pleasure, thus making it the common interest.

When one party does not experience adequate pleasure, the union itself becomes deficient. It could be said that there is no true sexual union taking place, but rather a form of masturbation by one party using the other's body. What makes the union a genuine sexual dynamic is the adequate pleasure experienced by both parties. Pleasure is the response to something particularly engaging occurring for oneself; an objective being reached.

The objective can be perceived as the pleasure itself or as the properties that generate this pleasure. When there is sufficient pleasure in a sexual dynamic, one can be assured that subjective development will follow. Just as one would be altered by engaging in a romantic experience, the same holds true for sexual experiences. It can be more perceptive to perceive the sexual objective as the properties that bring pleasure, rather than pleasure itself. When one does not understand the causation of pleasure, discussing pleasure alone would be fruitless.

Depression's Impact on Sexual Vitality

Although pleasure can be perceived as a self-focused neural response to sexual activity, there is a fundamental basis for its existence. An individual experiencing symptoms of depression would likely experience weaker sexual vitality. This is due to the mental narrative that depression gives rise to; once a state of affairs is assumed, the reproductive response becomes diminished.

We could propose that pleasure is still a nerve reaction, but this would not further our intellectual understanding. A better approach would be to suggest a logical reason for why the pleasure drive is lower in someone suffering from depression. Therefore, we can conclude that a depressed narrative has eliminated a sense of future progress. The perceived lack of progress may be the cause of the weakened sexual drive, which inherently focuses on a progressive future.

Thus, pleasure, in a sexual sense, is driven by the prospect of future progress. As we are naturally decaying, we seek to counter this process by engaging in actions that are directed toward the future; an extension of our disintegration. This becomes evident when we connect the idea of pleasure to the creation of a child, as both concepts are inherently linked. The outlook of a future human life is, in fact, the intellectual experience of pleasure.

Sexual Insight and Partner Dynamics

Sexual pleasure becomes possible when an individual senses a notion of the progressive future. Intimate sexual interaction serves as the means through which the progressive future is allowed to manifest. It is acknowledged that one cannot fully envision, enact, or engage with extreme opposing perspectives, even though these might offer a new approach. As a result, individuals seek sexual partners who possess the opposing insights they wish to develop.

Due to the intimacy involved in the interaction, there is inevitably an engagement with the partner's perspective. Given the level of intimacy, exchanging the most vulnerable bodily areas with the opposing partner, it is certain that the individual will gain the insight they seek. One such example might be the experience of pleasure itself, where one seeks comprehension into the experience of pleasure, and the other party offers insight into that knowledge. In this interaction, the individual perceives in the opposing partner an appreciation for aspects of selfhood they would not entertain on their own accord.

Attempting to gain this insight independently would cause an individual to lose their footing within the dynamic. The belief that one can existentially understand all the opposing elements of nature would prevent relationships from reciprocating experiential information; something that is fundamental to the very purpose of relationships.

Gendered Traits and Sexual Vitality

The attempt at procuring both gendered traits would lead to two outcomes: first, sexual vitality would wane, and second, one would yield the opposing characteristic that was overly sought. In fact, even the attempt to acquire the gendered trait that is antithetical to the core experiential state of the psyche would diminish the libido. This occurs because of the inherent experience of trying to embody both genders within a single individual, one that is more subjectively aligned with the person, and the other that is being attempted to be integrated into the psyche's substructure.

Weakened sexual vitality often drives the cause of seeking out new material to stimulate the exhausted libido. The act of seeking out new sexual material requires the psyche to unearth subtle information within the gendered traits, which can then be extrapolated for pleasure and dynamic connection. As a result, individuals embark on a sexual adventure, and as new information is integrated, they must find other sources of stimulation. The turnover rate is swift because these new roles and their associated information are not stimulating to the core subjective gendered state. The real issue isn't the sexual adventure itself, since dynamic learning is occurring, but rather that the weakened libido eventually abandons the pursuit of pleasure.

An individual may seek a sexual union with someone who embodies the gendered trait they neglect, deriving pleasure from reconnecting with the characteristic they have abandoned. This abandonment becomes a path to deep insight, awaiting rediscovery through intimate experiences. However, when seeking a partner to grant insight into the abandoned trait, they are essentially remaining intimate with themselves. Psychologically, the insight they hope to gain is already within them, so the union will feel like engaging in sexual intimacy with themselves. The opposing characteristic represents the highest form of sexual vitality, though it is, in reality, a neglected aspect of their own selfhood.

While the interaction may seem focused on the other person, there is a subconscious understanding of the participant already present within us. The partner acts as a catalyst, bringing to light subconscious material that has long been forgotten. Though they help illuminate this material, the experience will ultimately feel like an act of remembrance and nostalgia, as the gendered experience is something we have already known within ourselves.

Subconscious Knowledge of Gendered Traits

It can be argued that in all interactions, individuals are subconsciously aware of the gendered traits of their caregivers and will always mirror their sexual partner based on the known information. This can occur in any sexual dynamic without an external manifestation, as it pertains to the psychological state of each participant. However, there are distinct sexual dynamics: one that emphasizes developing memories and one that seeks a progressive learning experience.

For example, an individual who is psychologically cognizant may have mapped out an elaborate narrative of their childhood and, during a sexual union, may not consciously desire to highlight that. On the other hand, an individual who is psychologically cognizant but tussles with their childhood narrative may engage in a sexual dynamic in hopes of revealing more of the gendered traits that linger in their memory.

These intentions, whether related to grieving or mourning, are understandable. In such cases, a sexual union may aim to uncover aspects of the situation they are mourning. This sympathy persists even as we acknowledge the potential objectification, where the sexual participant becomes merely an object for revealing aspects of the mourning process.

The sexual engagement in which each participant explores the other, without serving as a mechanism to reveal subconscious material, takes place in a dynamic distinct from other types of interactions. A balance of removal and integration occurs, where there is an entering and exiting from this integration. When one participant takes an active step forward, the other falls back, and this alternates, with the second participant stepping forward while the first falls back. In this manner, the entire sexual interaction unfolds like a 'dance' of 'push and pull' until the final climax is reached. When there is a lack of this "dance" in the dynamic, it can be inferred that one or both participants are not exploring beyond themselves.

Hazards of Abandoning or Fixating on Characteristics

There is a sense of mystery that one would embrace to ensure that, even while seeking insight into the opposing characteristic, they do not abandon their own traits. What occurs is that the individual trusts the opposing party to offer that insight, without engaging outside of the sexual union.

The antithesis of this dynamic is when one becomes fixated on their own characteristics, which prevents them from seeking insight in the opposing trait. Yet, despite the dominance of sexual vitality, the individual will still engage in sexual unions, but the focus will shift toward gaining a more insightful perspective on their own traits. They will identify elements in their partner that highlight aspects of their own character, which, in turn, will cause them to fixate even more on those traits.

Similar to an individual who neglects their own character to the extent that they seek subconscious insight from another, the opposing extreme involves an individual who fixates on their own traits, seeking external validation from others. Both extremes result in individuals having an emotional experience of sexual intimacy by means of themselves; one with the neglected selfhood, the other with over-fixated selfhood. In both cases, the partners act as mediums for the ultimate climax with the self. Therefore, the partners are not the conclusion of the sexual union, but rather tools for intimacy with oneself.

This dynamic can be identified at the moment of climax, when the individual subtly pulls away slightly, allowing the final pleasure to arise. This contrasts with a climax that represents full integration, bringing about the experience of pleasure.

Achieving Balance in Sexual Dynamics

The balance between extremes lies in neither neglecting the natural characteristics arising from the depths of the psyche nor assuming that one's character is most perfected. Both the prideful and the exaggeratedly humble will fail to fully engage in the dynamic of a sexual union. For true pleasure to emerge, one must be open to conceding a privation in their own characteristics and remain receptive to the potential for greater insight.

At the same time, they would be amiss to abandon the characteristics that already exist within their psyche. This second condition may be difficult, as individuals may not be aware of such characteristics, which may remain dormant. This becomes apparent during a sexual union, where one might experience pleasure as either a "validating internal calm" or an "integrating development."

To ensure the sexual union is truly external to oneself, one must examine the process of the union. When both parties move slowly through the intercourse, but not excessively so, it signals that true perception is being gained. If the union happens too quickly, one can question the parties' motivations for rushing to climax. A desire for a quick climax might reflect an attempt to discover insight about their own character, which is already available contained by their psyche. Therefore, there is no need to rush the climax. In contrast, a slow and dynamic union indicates that each party is intrigued and in awe of the opposing character, genuinely astonished by a new perspective on being. With a methodical approach, the union will gradually integrate new insights and pleasures for both participants.

Pleasure ought to always feel different. If a sexual union produces the same type of pleasure, it suggests that the experience is not stemming from beyond the self. Pleasure derived from beyond oneself is always new and engaging because it presents something previously unknown. If the pleasure feels familiar, it indicates a reminder of past experiences for which the psyche has already encountered. If the learning experience had been fully integrated, one would not need to seek that dynamic again, as it is already part of their character. Thus, new pleasure demands new insights, and participants must confront innovative opposing characteristics relevant to their present moment.

At the most fundamental level, pleasure serves as sustenance, essential to the survival of the organism. It represents the futuristic notion of one's personal or biological continuation. Pleasure is simply the experience of "tasting" the completeness of life, which, when fully experienced, elicits satisfaction. The taste of food reflects the "taste" of one's future selfhood as it is consumed. Similarly, the pleasure of sexual intercourse symbolizes the "taste" of new human life, even when reproduction is unlikely. Likewise, even in the act of gluttony, food retains its taste. However, a third option must emerge. Each dynamic requires both parties to connect in such a way that one embodies a new persona.

The Role of Opposition in Learning

Based on the developments of one's life, their character assumes a position of learning, which always carries its shadow. To elicit a sexual response from the libido, one must seek the shadow, which is completely antithetical to their way of life. Not all learning will grant sexual pleasure, only those elements that are so opposite that only a complete, vulnerable integration will allow one to become aware of them. It is as though the learning that seems most completely lost will bring pleasure to an intimate union of bodies. The knowledge that appears lost in nature represents a form of expiry for the individual.

What can be solved through dialogue cannot occur in this situation. Having lost the possibility of learning through speech, action becomes necessary.

However, the action must be so intimate that each person reveals everything important to them and allows themselves to be fully intruded upon without any separation. The sexual dynamic represents the closest form of learning integration without becoming completely enmeshed. When complete enmeshment occurs, as in a codependent dynamic, all learning ceases because there is no distinct entity to receive the information.

The opposite could also occur, where the process is overly slow and sluggish. This suggests other intentions. The excitement of gaining an entirely new perspective should drive an individual to engage with its intricacies passionately. A lengthy ordeal suggests that such passion does not overtake the person because the sexual libido is weak.

Mystery, Confinement, and the Development of Sexuality

Oral fixation is thought to be a separate phase of sexual development, to which we must say that it is a byproduct of the realm of phallic sensory. For a lack of preliminary supposition of the sexual organ and its various usages, one views the oral arena, which is readily used and noted by its function, to be the metaphorical lens through which to undertake the intensity of sexuality that is found within the sexual organ itself. By being orally fixated, or for that matter, anally, it is the appropriation of the sexual organ and should not be considered distinct sexual aspects.

Sexuality is cumbersome with stimulatory responses which do not have a natural outlet and find themselves re-articulated in various manners, especially with other organs which have made their function quite available from the onset. We could say in this manner that the whole issue of sexuality is in terms of the fact that the sexual organ does not immediately become sentimental as a functional system. The lack of functionality shrouds mystery as to its effect, especially when its function is latent from the onset, such that normal development has one become suspicious of the organ but also existentially aware of its function. Had sexuality become functional from the onset, such mystery would cease to begin, and it would be similar to the function of the oral and anal organs.

Thus, sexuality is immediately thrust into a dual role of being existentially available, all the while awaiting the onset of bodily and mental development to become aware and proceed towards its functionality. In another way, we can view sexuality as the mystery of development, by the fact of confinement of the organ. The rest of the body is not confined toward its functionality, and without confinement, it proceeds on its path of inquiry with no separation between conscious and subconscious.

Such confinement brings mystery to the organ, and the more restricted sexuality is, the more mystery is to be entrusted to sexuality and the organ. We need only to look at young children who are exposed to the intricacies of sexuality—that is, the functionality of their organ and its use cases—to notice the diminished encasement of mystery, since the stage of confinement hadn't lasted the sentiment of "breaking free to sexual stimulation."

Although this seems like a positive step, for if the functionality of the organ has been studied at a young age, there is a loss of sexual stimulation. For the stimulatory response, very alike the tension of the organ through its function, requires that very confinement, and without such, the use of the organ is without sentimentality and thus viewed without stimulation. This is the same for any organ—in the case of the oral and anal capacity, without a sense of confinement, hunger, or necessity to defecate, it is without stimulation. That is, when one does not experience hunger or the necessity to defecate, there is a weaker stimulatory response to perform that function. The stronger the necessity—meaning the more confined the functionality of the organ is—the more stimulatory is its performance. Necessity is the modality of confinement, and that is what allows for the buildup of stimulatory tension, which upon release is noted as sexual pleasure but more so as its performance through that tension. With elasticity, the functionality ceases to perform. Therefore, mystery is the only matter of approach toward the sexual organ— that is, without undermining its confinement and thus removing the tension at the beginning of the process of releasing that tension.

Causes of a Weakened Libido

Even as a diminished sexual libido can have multiple causes, for our present discussion, it could stem from three primary reasons. First, the neglected characteristic of an individual is so acutely repressed that the excitement in revealing such is diminished.

Second, an overly fixated characteristic may be so intensely concentrated that further validation becomes unhelpful. This can also occur when the fixation involves perceived inadequacies that lack external affirmation, leaving no sense of perfection.

Third, the opposing characteristic may be perceived as threatening or too daring, placing the individual in a difficult position. By labeling the opposing characteristic as problematic, one essentially asserts that their own is not problematic, another form of an over-fixation upon the self.

Beyond these defects, a futuristic vision is also essential to a healthy libido, prompting one to seek insight into the opposing characteristic. When the future is grasped as problematic, the desire to envision such also fades.

Self-development is inherently tied to a vision of the future, as it involves progress from the current state to an improved one. Development is a movement from an inferior state toward a better, more evolved state. Therefore, the pleasure of sexual union lies in gaining comprehension for the future. When the future is viewed with disdain the libido diminishes.

Pleasure beyond Sexual Desire

The pleasure second only to sexual desire is the desire for sustenance, another futuristic notion that ensures survival. The most basic of these pleasures, consumption directly tied to sustenance, is typically the most consistently pleasurable. This also holds true in cohabitation, where the potential for children increases average pleasure.

Pleasure between two different forces arises as the result and purpose of their dynamic. A dynamic, by definition, is varied. This variation emerges from the interaction of the two partners and cannot be found in either alone. Through interaction, with each confined to a different perspective, they are forced to engage with the other perspective. Through this occurrence, one does not give up their own perspective nor disengage with the other perspective, so that a third option must emerge.

This third perspective will appear as the combination of the two but will also contain new aspects that cannot be deduced from the original perspectives. Therefore, the dynamic aspect of a relationship is the material that is not deductible from the sum of both parties.

Every dynamic has each party connecting so that, through that connection, each party becomes more wholesome. The demand for connection is the result of one wanting to be dynamical, recognizing the insufficient state of their isolated self. That recognition of insufficiency gives rise to the dynamic interaction, which causes one to become varied by the resulting third perspective. The pleasure is the new state both parties have gained, giving them a new perspective. Intellectually speaking, a new perspective is a new life, in that one is embodying a new persona. Thus, the pleasure can also be derived not only by the actual child resulting from the interaction but through the third perspective that grants novelty to each party.

The pleasure from a dynamic is more similar to the pleasure of sustenance than to the pleasure of sexual intercourse. The new life obtained from a dynamic relationship is an innovative intellectual life for each participant, similar to the new biological life owed to sustenance.

While one has gained life for the psyche, the other has gained in the body. Sexual intercourse, with its promise of a child, creates a newly formed biological entity that mirrors the parents. This new life is an external event, yet not external enough that it wouldn't be a manifestation of one's biological self. There is an element of biological continuity but also an element of complete externality, as the child lives without any assistance from the parents.

The new life of a dynamic and by extension of sustenance, occurs only within the internal realm, even though the elements that produced the new life are external. The new life comprising of a child occurs for the external realm, yet the core elements such as the semen and ovaries, which produced the new life, are completely internal.

Masculinity and Femininity in Dynamics

We may propose that in any dynamic, the two perspectives can be generalized in respect to their relationship of each other. These are not two individualistic perspectives which don't necessitate connecting material. The integrating process only occurs through the connecting material of the perspectives, which offers a reason as to why there is a need for integration. Not every perspective must be integrated to the result of a profounder third perspective, only those perspectives that are deemed necessary for integration.

The elements that cause a perspective to become necessary for integration are those that are felt to be lacking completeness. The second element that causes a perspective to become necessary for integration is those perspectives that are felt to be lacking direction and outline.

These two elements are the quintessential characteristics that demand the psyche to seek answers. However, all perspectives contain these two characteristics and should equally demand themselves for mediation. Instead, the perspectives that are experienced as completely lacking of either of these characteristics will be deemed the most appropriate for a dynamic. The perspective that is lacking the most will be deemed the most significant for a new perspective.

These two elements receive the names of masculinity and femininity, which will be characteristic of each perspective. Whatever the person of the dynamic comprises in their biological sense, the perspective that is most lacking, whether it is a lack of direction or completeness, will be the material that one brings to a dynamic. Yet, when both parties of a dynamic are seeking the same characteristic, what becomes of the dynamic is that one will take the opposing role so that the dynamic can be functional. This role-taking is only a temporary measure for a relationships to thrive.

Role-Taking and the Challenges in Dynamics

For the one who is only taking the role, secretly wanting to engage in the opposing characteristic, the experience will become disconcerting. The dynamic can reach a crucial stage in which the opposing party advances to the other characteristic, alleviating the pressure of the 'role-taker' by allowing the real need to manifest, thus fixing the entire dynamic. Between intimate partners, this switch must occur, and if it does not, resentment will form upon the party who is compelled to a certain role. Since people constantly shift along the masculine-feminine spectrum, these changes can occur rapidly.

Having one party take upon themselves the role, even if they are not situated in that particular characteristic, automatically causes the other party to enjoy their private characteristic in the dynamic. After a brief period of assuming the opposing role, the secondary party reveals their true nature, making them open to developing into the other characteristic. Meanwhile, the party taking on the role can revert to the characteristic that is more naturally suited to them.

The difficulty results in one of two stalemates: first, neither party is willing to take on a role opposite to what they truly need, or second, one party refuses to engage with a characteristic they essentially require. This leaves the participant assuming the role feeling exhausted by the other's reluctance to shift to the needed characteristic. The first issue arises when both parties are unwilling to 'act' for the relationship to maintain the dynamic, while the second occurs when one participant fails to recognize their own needs, something the other party can uncover through strategic maneuvering. By continuously switching between roles and factual characteristics, the dynamic can reset once the opposing party recognizes their true needs. This tactic requires ingenuity and patience, allowing the relationship to regain balance without outside intervention.

Masculinity, Femininity, and the Give-Take Dynamic

With an understanding of masculinity and femininity, we can further generalize by dictating that masculinity, previously described as a characteristic of direction, is a giver. Direction, as seen in a statesman offering guidance, does not directly benefit the one providing it. The content of direction does not yield benefits for the director in the areas being directed. The director stands inherently apart from the experience of being directed, occupying a position that does not interact with the outcomes of their direction. In a sense, the "market value" of direction lies in the complete detachment of the director from the situational aspect of being directed. As long as one is actively directing, they are not gaining from the act of directing, but only from incidental side effects. Thus, when one is engaged in directing, they are givers.

Alternatively, completeness, by its very nature, lacks an inherent leader or structure. To engage with the structure of completeness is to remove oneself from the experience of completeness and instead enter the realm of experienced direction. Therefore, to be in a state of completeness, truly for its own sake, it must be received from outside itself. To internally adopt a form of completeness is itself a form of direction and will fall short of full completeness. Thus, femininity, which we have associated with completeness, can also be seen as receiving. The reception must be complete for it to be considered feminine, just as the giving must be selfless in order for it to be considered masculine.

This presents another way to conceptualize masculinity and femininity: through a give-take dynamic. Upon further reflection, any give-take dynamic involves one party incorporated into the other.

Let's consider inanimate objects and their subtle sexual undertones. In light of this give-take view, a cup gives to the person who drinks from it. The drinker receives pleasure from the cup's delivery. This dynamic shifts when liquid is poured into the cup: the pourer brings pleasure to the cup, which now becomes the receiver. This illustrates how fluidly the masculine/feminine dynamic can shift. If the drinker is dissatisfied, the cup and its contents have failed in their purpose. Likewise, if someone pours carelessly and spills the liquid, they do not bring pleasure to the cup.

Instead of asking whether the inanimate cup "notices" a failure of masculinity, we focus on our emotional response to it. If a cup satisfies our needs, we may feel less emasculated than when we fail to pour liquid properly. Someone more attuned to femininity might feel more affected when the cup fails to meet their needs than when they fail to fill it. Thus, we are subtly influenced by sexual dynamics even in relation to inanimate objects.

Even though we don't perceive inanimate objects as capable of experiencing pleasure, our understanding is filtered through our own perceptions. We cannot grasp a state entirely devoid of pleasure, since all perception is rooted in an association of pleasure. We project the assumption that inanimate objects experience pleasure, even if we cannot know their actual state.

The Fallacy of Development

With sexual preoccupations at the root of life, this should be seen as straightforward and uncontroversial. The reason one might adopt a different view is what we can term "the fallacy of development" — the erroneous assumption that later stages of progress are not simply extensions of earlier ones. This fallacy may be reinforced by the belief that the present moment alone gives rise to phenomena, independent of the past, or that something outside the perceived realm gives rise to existence. For example, the fallacy would claim that a son is not merely an extension of his parents but exists on a wholly different plane. In truth, the son remains an extension of the parent while also being distinct and unique.

While we may not fully describe the factors that grant him this uniqueness, we assume it to be present. External factors like the environment and social surroundings also play a role in shaping who he becomes. Even so, these factors are themselves the result of other factors, allowing us to trace back to rudimentary elements that shaped the son's being. For instance, growing up in an upper-class environment will influence much of his condition. Yet we can trace such environments back to primordial behaviors found even in alpha chimpanzees, recognizing those roots in the fully formed human. (Sapolsky, 2017)[14]

Vitality and Mass: A Sexual Analogy

To further elaborate, we can take a theory in physics, which may seem abstract, and allow it to influence practical life. Einstein formulated that "mass and energy are both but different manifestations of the same thing... very small amounts of mass may be converted into a very large amount of energy and vice versa." This theory of reality can be understood to mean that all phenomena contain energy correlated to their mass and that, in essence, they are the same thing. It posits that everything is bound to energy in such a way that each incremental change in mass must also affect the amount of energy. Hence, an object of matter contains energy equivalent to the total amount involved in its creation. All phenomena derive from the singularity, a fatherly role, which, only through energy, continues to propagate throughout the universe in its later forms. Nature can be seen as the 'original father,' with countless energy, which then subdivides throughout existence while retaining pieces of the original father through its energy count.

We can take the most abstract concepts and subject them to a sexual framework to make them relatable. Splitting an atom, an abstract concept, can be understood through the framework of sexuality as a sadistic-masochistic dynamic. The process of splitting an atom through nuclear fission involves breaking apart the nucleus of an atom, which requires an immense amount of energy and pressure. Metaphorically, this process reflects a masochistic tendency, as it involves subjecting the atom to intense pressure and pain. When enough pain is inflicted, the atom emits a strong amount of sexual pleasure in the form of energy. In this dynamic, the sadist is the one who uses powerful technology to subdue the atom and break it apart. With enough pressure inflicted upon the atom, they succeed in releasing its immense energy. Therefore, through this lens, there is always a dynamic between the scientist and their work in nature. To further elaborate, we can take a theory in physics, which may seem abstract, and allow it to influence practical life. Einstein formulated that mass and vitality are both but different manifestations of the same thing... very small amounts of mass may be converted into a very large amounts of vitality and vice versa. This theory of reality can be understood to mean that all phenomena comprises vitality correlated to their mass and that, in essence, they are the same thing. It posits that everything is bound to vitality in such a way that each incremental change in mass must also affect the amount of vitality.

Hence, an object of matter contains vitality equivalent to the total amount involved in its creation. All phenomena derive from the singularity, a fatherly role, which, only through vitality, continues to propagate throughout the universe in its later forms. Nature can be seen as the 'original father,' with innumerable encapsulations of vitality, which then subdivides throughout existence while retaining pieces of the original father through its vitality count.

We can take the most abstract concepts and subject them to a sexual framework to make them relatable. Splitting an atom, an abstract concept, can be understood through the framework of sexuality as a sadistic-masochistic dynamic. The process of splitting an atom through nuclear fission involves breaking apart the nucleus of an atom, which requires an immense amount of vitality and pressure. Metaphorically, this process reflects a masochistic tendency, as it involves subjecting the atom to intense pressure and pain. When enough pain is inflicted, the atom emits a strong amount of sexual pleasure in the form of vitality. In this dynamic, the sadist is the one who uses powerful technology to subdue the atom and break it apart. With enough pressure inflicted upon the atom, they succeed in releasing its immense vitality. Therefore, through this lens, there is always a dynamic between the scientist and their work in nature.

The Problem with Full Sexual Liberation

The discussion now proceeds with sexuality as a central interpretive framework, one that not only reflects our subjective realities but also reveals the deeper structures determining social interaction.

The idea of liberating all sexual norms can never truly be considered genuine liberation. This is because sexuality is inherently ambiguous and rarely reveals itself in a straightforward way. When attempts are made to eliminate all power dynamics, the most aggressive behaviors often manifest in the bedroom. Sexuality, by its nature, involves a power dynamic. Unpacking what it means to be a power dynamic, one finds a giver and a receiver, so all sexuality contains this giver-receiver relationship.

When we choose to discard all sexual norms, we effectively remove this giver-receiver dynamic from the equation. The traditional union of man and woman, often representing that of a giver-receiver relationship, is relinquished, resulting in a confusing mixture of undefined givers and receivers.

If one partner gives or dominates without considering the pleasure of the other, they find no true enjoyment in the union. Similarly, the partner subjected to domination without experiencing pleasure will find the encounter distasteful. In such settings, the sexual drive can dissipate. When sexual desire is threatened, when one partner adopts a dominant posture that overwhelms the other's chance for pleasure, this dominion creates an imbalance. The dominant partner gains unmitigated access to the encounter, becoming a potent sexual force that may disregard their counterpart.

The Submissive Role and Balance of Power

The participant occupying the subordinate role of the union must adopt a voluntary submissive disposition to ensure an active role within this intimate engagement. Without active participation, where the state of vulnerability is consciously a sexual choice, the pleasure of the union will dissipate.

For the mutual agreement to be solidified, the participant in the submissive role can expect a certain concern from the dominant partner (sadist) in their vulnerable state, especially amidst the fragile landscape of their vulnerability. If the sadist ventures too far into sadistic inclinations, that is, if they take a disproportionate amount of space within the sexual union, the outcome may result in pain rather than stimulation.

We are accustomed to thinking of the sadist-masochist dynamic as a single partner inflicting pain for resultant pleasure, while the other receives pleasurable pain. However, what is occurring for each partner is a form of pleasure that can be perceived as pain from the outside.

The sadist, even with the most sadistic manifestations, endeavors to extract pleasure through the instrument of pain upon their sexual objective. Conversely, the masochist aspires to internalize pleasure through the experiential journey of receiving pain, as if this very pain unleashes a repository of pleasure.

Critical Sexual Theory

The Sadist-Masochist Dynamic

Against the conventional focus on the masochist's experience of pleasure in what appears to be pain, a far deeper inquiry concerns how the sadist finds pleasure when fully engaged in inflicting pain. This is especially significant considering that the pleasure seemingly arises solely from the masochist as a completely subjective experience.

However, when one actively inflicts pain that produces pleasure in their subject, the sadist, through intense immersion in the act, comes to share in the ultimate pleasure elicited by the masochist. In this interactive experience of pain, the sadist takes on the identity of the masochist, allowing the pleasure to be experienced subjectively. Through this identification, the sadist also experiences the pain they inflict, which paradoxically serves as a protection against an excessive amount of pain, all in pursuit of their ultimate pleasure.

Emotional Entanglement and Internalized Violence

Beyond sexual dynamics, when a person acts violently or aggressively with, they naturally begin to identify with the recipient and internalize the violence they inflicted. This emotional entanglement causes the states of aggressor and recipient to converge. Within sexual dynamics, the sadist, who engages solely in inflicting pain, gains no inherent benefit from the dynamic, while the masochist experiences pleasure as their primary function. The sadist depends on the masochist's pleasure for their own gratification, creating a dynamic where both parties anticipate mutual enjoyment. When this dynamic deteriorates to the point that the sadist fails to provoke pleasure in the other participant, the entire dynamic collapses into senselessness.

Although troublesome as an inquiry, an instance of sexual violence invariably culminates in a dearth of sexual gratification for all parties involved. Reported by victims, a notable proportion of assailants grappled with issues related to erectile inadequacy.[15] In the instances which result in satisfactory performance on behalf of the assailant, we may attribute this to the recipient having engendered a minuscule semblance of perceived pleasure.

The position of a sadist is to take the role of dominion, which inadvertently carries the expectation for the participant to embrace the role of subservience. When the role of subservience is not agreed upon, the dynamic becomes mutually inconclusive, demanding each participant to attend to a performative position for the dynamic to unfold. This situation results in the subservient party occupying a dominant role while anticipating a corresponding submissiveness from the other recipient.

The presence of power can always be found in an instance of sexual pleasure. We are referring to power as the assertion of existence in a dynamic fashion that allows a person's existence to permeate the social realm. The power is the readiness to exchange one's sexual vitality, defined by an experience of complete vulnerability through sexual intimacy.

The alignment of power with vulnerability becomes apparent when one exposes themselves to an intensified social interaction. Such intimate engagement during intercourse can be a profound interaction of pleasure and devastation or, conversely, an upheaval of one's perception of their own bodies or selfhood.

Power runs parallel with this dynamic in which, in a state of complete vulnerability, participants retain a willingness to engage with exuberant selfhood in relation to each other. Devoid of this power, the heightened level of vulnerability will render the interaction too daring. This power serves as a counterbalance to that vulnerability by allowing one to trespass the vulnerability of another while concurrently disregarding the heightened vulnerability of their own selfhood.

The Role of Masturbation in Sexual Dynamics

We cannot use individual sexual behaviors such as masturbation to contradict this assertion. Within oneself, there exists an imaginative role of partaking in a sexual union, even when the final act is physically performed alone. Some may conjecture that there are behaviors of masturbation that are purely sensual without an imaginative role. Yet if we explore all realms of the subconscious, we will surely find imagery assisting this act. Within those mnemonic images, we can always find a sort of union, even if it seems like a single individual for the image. Even the personal connection to that image becomes a sexual union; thus, an image that does not relate to the person will not elicit a sexual response. When one tries to master a sensual, meditative masturbation, they will create a sort of sexual union, and the two parties might be oneself and their sexual organs.

Critical Sexual Theory

The Illusion of Mutuality in Sexual Union

We must question the claim that the union between sexual parties is purely mutual, devoid of pain, obedience, and suffering. Unfortunately, this claim can be strengthened with evidence that the standard sexual interaction is consensual and mutual. We will ask both parties if they had wholeheartedly agreed to this interaction, and usually, we will get an affirmative yes. With this evidence, we will assume that normal sexuality is equal and fully pleasurable, without dominion and pain. We believe this is a mistaken notion of the concept of mutual and consensual.

We can mutually agree to experience pain and still define it as a consensual union. Because there is a consensual union does not mean that there is no pain. Even with the seemingly painless sexual union, where heightened pleasure is experienced, we miss the intricacies of that experience. We know this to be true by the overestimation of a partner in a sexual union, where we often fail to notice things that would usually disgust us. Very commonly, couples will exchange saliva but will not share a toothbrush.

This overestimation will also lead to overestimate the experience as being purely pleasurable, devoid of pain and dominance. So that the child who experiences their parents cohabitating will interpret the scenario as a form of aggression. They will begin to become more aggressive by example and will not notice the pleasure associated with that aggression. For the child, they are seeing pain and dominance, so that the one who is cohabitating is also experiencing pain and dominance. They might not notice it because of the heightened pleasure that overrides the dominance, but it is still present and noticed. Furthermore, we can assert that dominance and pain are predecessors to pleasure. Pleasure is a result of the dominance; without dominance, there will be no pleasure.

The Influence of Passive Experiences

Upon further introspection, we find pain and dominance present in nearly every activity or experience one encounters. Even cleaning one's living space involves pain; even those predisposed to tolerate it will not clean without the purpose of eventually experiencing cleanliness. They will not clean a street casually, and if they do, it won't be a street from another town. Since some pain is inherent in the task, there must be a justification that makes that pain worthwhile. The items and spaces to be cleaned become dominating entities over the individual who furnishes them with full attention. The floor dominates the cleaner so long as it requires cleaning.

The person can dominate the floor by choosing to ignore cleanliness and could remain so for an extended period. The problematic nature of an unclean living space will manifest, and still, the person can ignore that in order to remain in the dominant position. Once they engage with the floor in cleaning its surface, the notion of cleanliness and the floor become domineering participants until the task is completed.

Surely, we can surmise from this example that dominion is not a terrible thing but a reality of life, which can assist a person even with their subjugation. A clean living space assists in the quality of life while that objective of cleanliness dominates one's life. The sexual union, being an interaction between two entities, will always contain an element of dominance. Just as the clean room cannot occur without the room taking the role of dominant party, so too requires one party in the sexual union to be dominating and one party to be subservient. If either both parties neglect to take the role of dominion or neglect to take the role of subjugation, the sexual pleasure will dissipate.

The Limits of Mutuality in Pleasure

The only availability of pleasure in such a union lies in the realm of masturbation, that is, the imagery of a sexual union. If the experience becomes truly mutual, it results in another form of masturbation. Each party remains distant from the other, and only through the aid of imagery can they generate an experience of pleasure. When they move beyond this form of mutuality and seek an actual sexual connection, one party must assume a dominating role while the other takes a submissive role.

Confusion arises when someone chooses a role contrary to their natural sexual proclivity. By choosing a role, they distance themselves from the sexual pleasure that could be derived from the union. Since all sexual pleasure stems from the pain within the power dynamic, the pleasure experienced in a chosen role is diluted. They are merely acting out the role rather than living the experience itself. The actor will not gain the same pleasure as the one naturally situated in that role. Moreover, by taking a role rather than embodying it, one seeks only the pleasure from the union and neglects the union itself. Pleasure is only a derivative of the union, and when one bypasses the union to pursue pleasure directly, they neglect both the union and the pleasure.

Additionally, the submissive party being dominated will always seek to maintain a consensual nature. Nonetheless, even in the most forceful situations, one can preserve a degree of autonomy by actively participating in the interaction. By simply engaging with what is occurring, even when there is no apparent choice, a sexual dynamic can still exist between the two parties. Engagement with the world always involves some source of pleasure, and seemingly unpleasurable activities can be connected to a source of pleasure.

Playing an active role in an unpleasurable experience provides pleasure through the mastery of one's abilities within the interaction. This helps explain why some are drawn to entertainment that is horrific or distressing, the active role they assume grants them pleasure. The formula for a total absence of pleasure is an unpleasurable experience combined with complete passivity, which ultimately undermines the dynamic of the relationship as a whole.

The Impact of Passive Engagement

Seligman's study teaches us that what occurs is a disengagement from reality: "Animals subjected to repeated and uncontrollable shocks, when placed in a new situation in which they could take action to terminate the shocks, fail to learn to do so. They become passive, with a learning deficit that is not due to any apparent sensory or motor deficit. They have learned that nothing they do matters and that whatever happens is out of their control" (Seligman, 1975).[16]

The damage of the dynamic, where one cannot take an active or pleasurable role, creates a disconnect from reality. The nihilistic abyss that is created means that there is no purpose for the party's engagement, neither being pleasurable nor serving as active engagement. Yet, they are still forced to remain in some sort of participation within the dynamic. When studied enough, that small amount of participation can provide a sense of pleasure. We cannot disengage completely from our dynamics of pleasure and reality.

When a sexual dynamic results in a complete lack of autonomy, besides the neglect of pleasure in the interaction, the sexual dynamic itself becomes deflated and worthless. Nature is structured so that there is always a dynamic interaction between forces. When one party does not experience this dynamic as autonomous, the engagement from the other party diminishes, causing the dynamic itself to fade.

In a civilization founded on complete sexual liberation, all citizens would collectively agree to eliminate the need for consensual agreements. Every sexual impulse would be freely expressed, supported and enforced by social norms and laws. These norms would demand that every individual liberate their sexual impulses and would not accommodate those who resist such expression.

The Implications of Sexual Norms

'Rights' will align with those who express their sexuality rather than those who refuse such advances. Hence, the most sexually liberated societies will also be deflating the overall sexual dynamic. With the social norm being sexual liberation, people will sexually engage as per the norms, while they subconsciously oppose the interaction.

This will result in a deflated sexual dynamic for both parties, and as such, the entire society will neglect their sexual duties. Another possibility could occur, as we have seen with the people of Pre-Contact Hawaii. Sexuality becomes removed from the personal realm. Amy Stillman writes, "Sexuality in pre-contact Hawaii was closely linked to concepts of power, hierarchy, and the exchange of goods and services," thus sexuality was exchanged as a matter of commerce. For political purposes, "Sexual relations between high-ranking individuals, including chiefs and their consorts, were often seen as a way to establish political alliances and maintain social order." (Lilikalā Kameʻeleihiwa).[17]

We can demonstrate this with a graphic study of their intercourse, completely devoid of foreplay, denoting a disengagement in the *loving* aspect of intercourse. "According to the reports of Westerners of pre-contact Hawaii, extensive foreplay was not a standard part of coitus. Many reports and stories tell of an adult male and an adult female meeting on a trail in the bush or on a secluded beach and engaging in coitus immediately, with little conversation and few preliminaries" (Marshall).[18] What can result from a sexually liberated society is either a decrease in sensuality or a disconnection from the emotional engagement with sex.

The Libido

The libido is individualistic and cannot partake in communal reciprocity of connectivity. Even though a social being can connect to various aspects of nature, those pathways of connection and their resulting objects are not necessarily bound to the libidinal atmosphere. There should be no major surprise regarding what halts the libidinal drive along these connection pathways, and even more so, what distinguishes non-libidinal connections.

Let us begin by way of example and build a theory of libidinal connectivity and its parameters. Imagine the connective pathway as an object of nature, corresponding to a specific tree. We cannot deny the validity of that connection, which is felt so deeply that leveling the tree would cause melancholic symptoms akin to genuine mourning. However, we would also be aware of a lack of libidinal drive contained by the connection, and if such a drive were found, it would stretch the limits of our imagination.

What is lacking in the tree that cannot stimulate the libidinal urge? First, we must examine the connection itself to determine what causes the initial attachment to a tree. We may find that it represents an aspect of nature with a particular characteristic that marks it distinct among its peers. We can acknowledge this by finding a person with a connection to a tree, someone who may have no particular connection with nature. This would be difficult to explain: what is so particular about a tree that is not shared by the rest of nature? Whatever characteristic of the tree stimulates a connection would likely be available throughout nature.

The tree can have a symbolic or associative representation that stimulates the connection. The connection is made through these associative measures, like sharing a relationship to its location. Associative connections do not display anything inherent and rely entirely on the association for their stimulation. We could imagine a libidinal drive toward a person based solely on such associations, for example, someone resembling another person. Yet within the connection itself, there are distinct characteristics separate from the association. These are the aspects of the connection that could stimulate the libidinal urge, while the association serves as an imaginary stimulus.

We can view the tree's connective characteristic as emblematic of nature as a whole. Nature is sought for many reasons, foremost among them its relation to the fundamental states of personhood, offering a sense of peace by allowing one to rest in their innate being, free from mental abstractions.

The wholesomeness of nature is relatable to the wholesomeness of personhood. The distinguishing factor of this particular tree lies in its specific aspects of that natural state of existence. The tree may be the 'bearer of fruit,' the 'one which branches out in many pathways,' or it may evoke a sense of 'humility' or a 'sheltering' characteristic that offers a sense of home. All these examples are specific aspects of the overarching nature that relate to the rudimentary state of personhood.

When contrasted with this, the libidinal drive does not relate specifically to any particular object. Rather, the entire class of gendered-sex stimulates the drive, and a specific object is approached through that connection. Gendered-sex serves as the stimulating connection for many reasons, including its relation to one's own gender. The opposition of the gender becomes highlighted as something authentic, similar to how nature opposes personhood by being a non-abstract form of existence. Had nature been an abstract form that also contained elementary aspects of existence, it would be called human.

The human being is not as relatable as nature because they lack a 'non-abstract opposing' characteristic, as if nature beckons one to follow her path against the natural stream of human flourishing. The opposing gendered-sex calls one to follow their innate nature, an awareness of complete personhood. Had it been the psychologically identical gendered-sex, it would not beckon personhood because it lacks opposing characteristics. The opposition is merely a method for engagement, which ultimately becomes non-gendered. Gender is only a stimulus to relate, while the true connection is the relatability of all human aspects despite specific genders.

Nature, Personhood, and the Libidinal Drive

We have not yet advanced our inquiry into why the libidinal drive is stimulated only by certain connections. The distinguishing factor becomes clear when contrasted with the previous example: nature offers only a partial relatability to specific aspects of personhood, while leaving others untouched. One who becomes completely enmeshed with nature, as we are aware some do, would lose hold of the fuller, developed notion of personhood. Human relations, however, differ, because gendered-sex serves as an object of relation to the entirety of personhood, including nature itself. No aspect remains untouched by this relational influence.

Nature would stimulate the libidinal drive if it encompassed the entirety of personhood. The parameter of the libidinal drive is complete relatability to personhood; the closer an object comes to fulfilling this criterion, the more stimulating it becomes within the libidinal atmosphere. Even so, these partial connections can contribute to the finality of a libidinal urge. The imagination and the physical environment surrounding cohabitation can be enriched by these secondary connections, offering a more stimulating overall experience. Thus, the element of nature highlights the rudimentary states of personhood, while the human partner offers what lies beyond, that is, the complete state of personhood.

For instance, sexual activity within nature allows certain aspects of personhood to be highlighted. Technically, sexual stimulation between persons is wholly self-sufficient and requires no external elements to provide stimulation. However, relating to personhood without engaging its various aspects through an external venue is quite difficult. Therefore, we rely on external processes, which form part of the perceptual experience, to be integrated into the sexual union, thereby highlighting these dimensions of the relationship.

When we enter the human realm of sexuality, we encounter situations where the relatability of each partner does not call forth a complete state of personhood. Pederasty, for example, clearly reflects a lack of full relatability to complete personhood. Boyhood cannot fully relate to the entirety of adulthood, just as adulthood cannot fully relate to boyhood, as it lies beyond its realm of understanding. This raises the question: how can there be a libidinal urge in such a case, when the connection is only partial?

The imaginative realm is quite expansive and can entertain what is not aligned with perception and reality. The difference between boyhood and adulthood is not as vast as one alongside nature, and with some abstraction, it could be perceived as an all-encompassing connection.

The distinguishing divisions are blurred when the object of relatability is closer to that all-encompassing characteristic. For instance, when there is young adult in relation to mature adulthood, it becomes difficult to identify differences. The social environment may puzzle over a couple with a major age gap, wondering how this 'partial' connection has become all-encompassing. Furthermore, there is a sense of discontent as the knowledge that one is using a 'partial' connection to entertain the libido troubles the social environment. There is concern that one would abuse the libidinal drive with partial connections.

Secondly, there is discontent at a declining environment in which one is unwilling to relate to complete personhood, accepting partial relatability. The lines of demarcation are understood by the subjective realm, while in cases where the object is fairly different, it would be clearly understood by all.

Therefore, we can conclude that the libidinal drive exists alongside every connection. However, the onset of a libidinal expression will only be found when the connection offers a kind of relatability that is all-encompassing to personhood. Gendered-sex is a method that beckons a connection by being in psychological opposition and likewise completely relatable to every aspect of personhood.

Consciousness and the Libidinal Drive

In this discussion, we will define consciousness as a sense of awareness. When one is fully engaged in consciousness, they are not available to experience an awareness of personhood itself. Having assumed this awareness as already attained, there is nothing further that the gendered-sex could contribute. Therefore, an awareness, or a presumed awareness, of selfhood is always antithetical to the libidinal drive, which relies on aiding the emergence or elevation of consciousness. When one is already firmly situated within the realm of consciousness, sexual connection becomes unnecessary.

Thus, the availability to experience personhood is a prerequisite for the libidinal urge. However, we might imagine that even in the presence of a presumed awareness of personhood, a particular sexual scenario could still evoke a libidinal response. In such cases, the sexual stimulus overrides the perceived awareness by asserting itself as overtly sexual, that is, by implicitly claiming a "lack of awareness" concerning the sexual dimension. This creates the possibility of sexual arousal despite an inclination toward conscious self-sufficiency. Yet such arousal would require a stronger or more explicit stimulus to compel a sexual response.

Ideally, the mere presence of gendered-sex should provide sufficient stimulus to activate the libidinal drive, by virtue of its partial opposition to the self. To introduce a dynamic element into the situation, one must assume incomplete self-knowledge, a lingering darkness within the self. Mystery can only exist when there is a perceived unknown in which that mystery may reside. When everything is presumed to be fully known, neither mystery nor the natural libidinal urge can arise.

Libidinal Drive and Selfhood

The libidinal drive depends as much on relatability as it does on its ability to foster self-awareness of personhood. Relatableness can be disturbed either by a disparity between the object of connection and the self, or by a lack of connection to selfhood itself. This may seem paradoxical: when there is complete relatability to selfhood, there shouldn't be room for another sexual object to evoke a new sense of self-awareness. Yet without any initial relatability to selfhood, there would be no 'self' requiring awareness in the first place. Thus, the libidinal urge requires both a basic sense of self and an openness for discovering a new dimension of that self. Where there is neither an initial self-awareness nor a readiness for self-discovery, the libidinal urge would appear unnecessary.

This is not a simple matter of understanding what it means to relate to oneself. By definition, being within oneself should suggest an ongoing, consistent relatability. How, then, could one become disconnected from their own self-relation while still maintaining some form of personhood? To address this, we must ask where the notion of relatability is situated in regard to personhood. Which is more fundamental: does personhood necessitate relation, or does relation demand the presence of an expansive person?

Regardless of how this question is resolved, we can move forward in our analysis. Rather than determining the ultimate foundation, we may accept that both are essential to personhood. The way one becomes relatable to oneself depend entirely on how the surrounding environment initially related to them. We can imagine a scenario in which no external beings or phenomena share existence with us—essentially, an island presence devoid of any matter that reflects our own being. In such a state, the development of relatability would be impossible.

In this case, our sense of existence would lack a center; we would not even be able to distinguish between experiences of pain or pleasure. It would be as if we stood as mere onlookers to ourselves—though even this would be insincere, since the very notion of being a third-party observer requires prior familiarity with differentiation. Therefore, the capacity for self-relatability is inextricably bound to the presence of external realities in relation to us.

Libido and the Primacy of Moments

The libido level should be an interesting inquiry if we are to understand sexuality as a whole. We should not assume that sexual vitality, what we are terming libido, is expressed laterally; rather, it should be viewed as a spectrum. There is a form of libido that consumes much of the embedded persona, and another that scarcely reveals itself. This spectrum fluctuates across many scales of analysis, from the minute to the decade. One might experience both a high and low point in their libidic spectrum across the span of a day, while also encountering broader fluctuations over the course of their life. As one ages, libido tends to decrease, suggesting that this spectrum is not as random as we may have thought. Hayes (2005) found a tendency for women's sexual function to decline with age, beginning in the late 20s to late 30s. Specifically, desire, frequency of orgasm, and frequency of sexual intercourse decrease with age.

If such a tendency can be identified on a broader scale, we may be able to locate libidic fluctuations within the rhythms of the day, week, month, and year. Winter is a time of possibly heightened libidic vitality, for instance, being the season in which most conceptions occur. The weekend could be seen as the point of highest libidic energy of the week, and night as the peak of the day.

The adult represents the prime of life; the weekend, the primacy of the week. The night is similarly primal, "What are you doing tonight?" carries more significance than comparable questions about other times of day. Winter, however, stands at odds with these examples: while summer is typically regarded as the height of the year.

The higher rate of conception in winter may not be due to heightened libido but rather to environmental conditions that enable successful procreation. The climate of winter encourages people to retreat into domestic spaces that offer safety and warmth. This "cave" facilitates a calm and settled atmosphere where pregnancy can begin. The body becomes relaxed and receptive to the enduring process of gestation. Procreation is more likely to be considered in a space of quiet and stillness. Summer may, in fact, be the high point of libido, but its restlessness might inhibit conception. The body might resist it, and the mind, recognizing the unsuitable conditions, could consciously or subconsciously circumvent conception, such as by tracking ovulation to miss the event.

Sexual vitality, then, is linked to the culmination of periods within the celebratory phase of life. This becomes understandable if we view the libido as an expression of procreation. When one reaches the height of life, they are reminded of the desire to extend themselves into future generations. Heightened sexual vitality would be premature for someone who has not yet reached maturity. This vitality diminishes as the individual, or the week, winds down; when the time for offering oneself to further generations has passed. At those intervals, one regresses, and it becomes untimely to continue sexualizing the self.

Thus, the libido appears most active in moments of primacy, as if the importance of a moment summons libido into action. The supremacy of a moment is marked by the culmination of mundane affairs. We are interested in the weekend because it concludes the motion of the week, asking, "How are you celebrating your week?" The adult stands at the prime of life, a culmination of childhood and adolescence.

The spectrum of sexual vitality is found in the primacy of moments. Yet, as conscious beings, we choose what is important and what is not. The arbitrator of what holds standing gives us some control over our sexual vitality. For instance, while the weekend is widely understood as the culmination of the week, an individual may place personal significance on another day, an anniversary, holiday, or event, which may heighten libido. However, this heightened value arises from our designation of importance. We control the hierarchy of moments and, by extension, influence our sexual vitality.

We have discussed that heightened sexual vitality arises from the primacy of life. Let us now extend this idea: the primacy of life is, to a degree, under our control, and the libido will respond to such regulation. The libido declines in mundane and simplistic moments, and intensifies in heightened ones. This can become problematic if the weekday does not serve to culminate at the weekend. For someone to find all the value in the mundane of their life, there can be no celebration for its development. Much like living in early adolescence, which is a preparatory phase of development toward adulthood, one may wonder about a weakened libido vitality. There must be a narrative cycle that interchanges the simplistic moments with the heightened moments.

In truth, we can scale this concept within a single day, which contains both heightened and mundane moments. The structure of the day should allow the mundane to serve the night, making the day's experiences meaningful. The night receives the day's work, and the libido is contextualized therein. To increase one's sexual vitality, one must culminate the day. First, they must stop the mundane tasks; second, they must absorb the experiences of the day. This attitude resembles that of a holiday. Such a mindset becomes a generalization of life, taking in the moment, the beauty, and the sensuality of things. Sensuality parallels sexual vitality; it is, in many ways, an abridged version of the holiday or weekend. One cannot remain immersed in daily tasks while maintaining sensual awareness. Even the sensual person must occasionally step back from the sweetness of things in order to broaden their perspective.

We could imagine that one who has experienced war may not appreciate war-themed art or film. Such works aim to bring awareness to an experience that is already embedded in the viewer's consciousness. A connection to art has its purpose in culminating to a previously unattended experience.

Sensuality is based on culminating experiences, and sexual vitality follows suit. The libido will be energized by mindsets which culminate in experiences, and most sexual fantasies pertain to that. The final act of sexuality is also a culmination, denoting that we must maintain a generalized mindset that can culminate to a final experience in order to energize the libido.

Relating to Others and the Mirror-Self

With this setting established, relating to oneself becomes no different from relating to others. The only reason there is a heightened potency in self-relation is because of the external insistence present from the very first moments of life. For example, when a communal body erodes its members' sense of individuality, the framework of relatability within that insular environment positions the individual as something other than the center of their own universe. This assumption becomes internalized at the deepest levels, to the point that pain inflicted upon the community is felt as keenly as personal pain.

However, physical pain still attests to a certain centrality that cannot be experienced with the same depth in a communal sense. Yet even physical pain arises and is registered within a matrix of deeply embedded memories of environmental relatedness; memories that first taught the individual about their own skin. We could imagine a scenario in which, from the very first moments of life, an individual is conditioned by the environment to believe that the self is not a standalone entity. In such a case, it is possible that physical pain would not be felt *as an individualistic sense*. One could even argue that the physical pain seemingly experienced at birth is not truly pain, but rather a systematic expression of stimuli reaching a certain threshold.

Laughter, Crying, and Relating to the Self

Laughter and crying are biological expressions directed at safeguarding individuality. However, this is a learned trait shaped over many generations of development. Initially, it would not necessarily have been the case that such biological expressions served to protect the entity itself. In other words, the entity may once have been defined by a larger setting, one that we would not even recognize as an 'entity' in the familiar sense. For example, we might encounter an organism that does not seek its own protection but rather the protection of something other or greater than itself. Yet because, from the outset, most organisms were related to by the environment as discrete, original entities, this became the criterion of personhood.

We might wonder about the original condition, whether the environment truly 'chose' to relate to organisms as individual entities, or whether this was a mistaken abstraction. In this sense, human beings relate to themselves in the same manner they relate to others, a device or mechanism employed more consciously by some than by others.

Let us explore how one relates to another, as this will shed light on how one relates to oneself. The manner in which one relates to another is through an active engagement in a mirror-like experience, wherein the other highlights specific aspects of selfhood. For example, another person may wear a particular style or color that elicits certain sentiments within the self, sentiments that are brought to awareness through this mirrored relation.

Therefore, in relation to oneself, the process is similar. We can divide the self into two parts: one is the avatar who performs the act of relating, and the other is the object of relation. This may seem unusual or unfounded, but by becoming a persona of observation upon selfhood, one is able to relate to oneself. We will call the one doing the relating the 'inquiring-self', and the other the 'object-self.' The inquiring-self seeks material from the object-self by finding things it can relate to. If one assumes that nothing is unknown within the entirety of selfhood, then the self cannot be divided into two distinct arenas, one seeking to know the other.

The truth is that we never know the entirety of selfhood at any moment. When one side of the self takes the role of exploring the other, it is not exploring known territory. For example, the inquiring-self might find the present experience relatable to a certain memory. The object-self, simply performing life's tasks, is unaware of this sense of experience. Thus, there is a sense of darkness upon the object-self, which the inquiring-self notes and attempts to relate to something else. This culminates in an experience of relating to oneself.

Sexual Expression

There is a method to deal with the sexual impulse in which the mental capacities are used up to a point where the instinctual aspects lose their expressive nature. The mental arena can control instincts not only through present self-restraint but also by subjugating the drive with mental rhetoric. This rhetoric can exist in both conscious and unconscious forms but stems from the same source, the mental arena subjugating the organic drives which see their aim solely in expression.

Let us be precise in explaining how a certain biological component, such as the mind, can take on an organic structure and dismiss its expression upon personhood. Instincts arise from a different avenue, and even though they are linked with the mental capacity, they are sourced from organic matter, one which does not require a brain to form itself. We can argue that the sexual instinct was present at an early stage of life, with cell reproduction as its source. In any case, when the brain and mental capacities developed, they did so against the backdrop of the preliminary sexual drive and surrounding organic structure.

According to this supposition, there should not be an available mechanism in which mental capacities can override pre-mental organic structure. However, the mind has access to every aspect of the organic structure, not in its intrinsic state but in a powerful representation. The intrinsic organic structure is standalone in its full form without the mind having the power to alter any part of it. The point of control lies in utilizing the organic material for the mental representation of the psyche. We are only concerned with mental representation, for that is the mode of reality we are used to. Behind the walls of this representational psyche lies a perfectly formed sexual instinct which, in its own sense, expresses itself in a normal fashion. The expression is constantly outflowing in the same manner, though its final representational form can be convoluted as per the mental capacity stipulations.

Part Two: Sexuality

This is why Freud assumed that the sexual instinct will prerequisite its expression no matter the scenario, and when submerged, will be the occasion for sublimation. This implies that the perfect instinct, upon arriving to the mental representation, takes on a new form where there is some logical sequence. The mind will not be able to represent the sexual instinct in a way that must be understood if the sequence of thoughts were mapped out.

The specific connection between repression and the core instinct is somewhat organic but of a lower kind. The initial representation seeks to portray the organic features as accurately as possible. This aligns with the core thesis of the mind: to represent in an accurate form so as to deal with the complexity of the organic structure. The initial representation arrives, and a logical continuity emerges, allowing the mind to begin handling the material counter to the organic aspects.

However, the mind must adhere to one rule: it must follow a coherent logical sequence from the organic material into whatever realm it seeks to pass in. This is a safety mechanism for both the organic structure and the mind, preventing them from becoming so disjointed that they no longer serve the same purpose. Thus, the mind adheres to a core tenet of unity upon which every mode of activity is formed through a logical continuum.

For the mind to sublimate the sexual instinct, it must find something of greater importance, worthwhile enough to offer up the pure reproduction rights. Freud mentioned intellectual pursuits as an example, where we can assert a logical argument for those pursuits at the cost of sexual aims. However, we would not be able to transfer the instinct to something that is not equivalent or in logical order with the sexual instinct.

The caveat to the mental ability to represent sexuality in any manner it can logically formulate is the organic structure itself. From its perspective, the organic structure seeks reproduction in the form of absolute sexuality. When it sees that the mind has made use of the instinct in a way that neglects its aim, it finds avenues of conflict. These aspects of the organic structure, which seek a more wholehearted version of sexuality, can enter the mind's representational forum as new forms of thought. They do not enter as new forms of sexuality, as the major sexual drive has already been covered in the sublimation process. They would lose representational relevance if they entered under the pretext of new forms of sexuality, and more importantly, they cannot do so because the drive itself already holds representational value.

They thus enter as a point of conflict rehabilitated as representational aspects that enact a small portion of the sexual instinct left over in them. Their only ability, besides the sexual drive, is that they are the more important organic matter. So they enter in representational form as undisclosed organic matter which takes the place of continuity in the psyche, simply by being something more significant.

The Symptoms of Conflict

These disruptions, simply by being present, naturally interrupt the mental flow, as they are the material itself and always hold more relevance than its representation, even though they appear as solitary. The symptoms show up as gaps in logical sequences. These organic intrusions lack logic, being biological in nature. Two effects lead to the final symptom: First, the gap in the logical flow creates a sense of non-logical matter, essentially an empty void, devoid of meaning, substance, or relevance. It essentially becomes an existential gap. The symptom manifests as this experience, with varying responses depending on the individual. Inquiring into the material of this gap usually leads to a form of nihilism.

The second cause of the symptom is that the psyche perceives itself as a faulty system. The mind is concerned with losing its representational cohesiveness, as raw material has entered its space. In a sense, the mind no longer feels safe with its own system, representing this sentiment as a threat to the entire biological system.

These strands of thought related to the symptom, or more accurately to the neglected organic material, can then be used in many different ways in order to weaken its effect on oneself. It can be neglected, sublimated again, subjugated, or dealt with in other ways, all which provide a sense of safety to the system. Therefore, the symptom arises as organic matter in its representational form to which, instead of it entering as the material of the organic structure itself, creates many problems for the psyche, as mentioned above.

Interactions between Organic and Mental Structures

Even though the drive itself is managed by the mind, it still has to allocate for the other aspects of the organic structure which seek to advance conflict with the sublimation state. In this way, there is an indirect dialogue between the organic matter and the mind, for when its expression does not make its way towards the objective, it will form counter-representational models, which become an aspect of conflict until the situation is settled. The symptoms arise from those aspects of the organic structure and cannot be logically traced to the representation of the sexual instinct itself.

This would also mean that expressing oneself in a more open sexual fashion would not wane the symptoms. There are specific aspects of sexuality that have been neglected, and allowing them to integrate into the full spectrum of sexuality would introduce organic matter, which then becomes the cause of symptoms. These have very particular and intricate details based on the organic structure in its absolute form. More liberal sexuality will usually not be a pathway for rebalancing the organic structure alongside the psyche. In this way, the post-Freudian world has evolved toward a more open sexual society, based on the assumption that this openness would alleviate the symptoms. The first task is to uncover the fundamental organic structure and then to understand how the psyche has been subjugated to a point where the organic periphery causes disruptions.

The Disruption of the Psyche and Organic Structures

It can be traced, as we have done, but we cannot directly connect the mental material of symptoms to the sexual instinct itself. When the situation shifts toward a more satisfactory state for the organic structure, those messengers, whose sole purpose was to represent themselves disruptively in the psyche, will be removed. Therefore, we cannot claim that the symptoms are an inherent part of the organic structure of the body or even the psyche; they exist solely to restore balance between the psyche and organic matter.

The interesting aspect of this interactive map between the organic and the psyche is that the representational forms of the marginalized organic matter can externally manifest. The sole aim is to be represented, and this can happen in external forms which are entered via perception. For instance, this is quite characteristic in intellectuals who, while making use of some organic sexuality for their pursuits, develop a certain distaste for sexual interest. For them, these forms of sexual interest are the representational aspects of the neglected aims of sexuality. This distaste arises in the same way that symptoms emerge in the internal system, only now, it is the perception-externality that embodies the organic matter.

One may wonder why this distaste occurs, as the issue now seems external rather than an internal mishap. The external form embodies the organic matter in its representational form, and when facing oneself, it becomes the gap of the psyche to which the individual relates to that social-externality. The sexual interest becomes an external embodiment of the entire internal process of the symptom. The same empty void, which constitutes the organic matter that intruded upon the mind, is perceived in the direction of the sexual interest. It becomes equivalent to the existential threat experienced in the psyche, and is often disliked for that reason. In fact, a strong sense of detestation may arise, which, upon understanding the process, becomes logically ordered. This interest is as disruptive to the psyche as a threat to its system, embodying the material of existential deadness in a social form.

This is similar to the young body who suffers the girl he likes because she represents the latent sexual matter that has not been adequately represented for the psyche. The child hates her just as he would hate any psychological symptom or nihilistic expression.

There is a secondary abhorrence that applies only to the external forms of this representation of the marginalized organic matter. They also represent, to perception, the reality of the situation and the impossibility (or possibility) of relief. By being material for perception, they create a more wholesome reality that highlights the internal conflict by way of more evidence. The girl for the young boy represents the inability to perform a physiological solution, as she is the opposite of real sexuality, which is assumed to be a failed attempt. She also represents the possibility of absolute expression, which the boy acknowledges as something he cannot achieve in the present moment.

Using an external form to represent organic matter is largely due to an individualized perspective. For someone who seeks to align the psyche with the social environment and is more communal or political in nature, would surely make use of an external reference point for this internal process. They might do this in a socialized manner, with only a slight hint of deeper revulsion. This is quite special, as such revulsion, especially considering all the nihilistic thinking that arises, would be controlled to an off-putting remark, which is a testament to the power of social learning and communal influence upon the individual.

There is also the fact that one can recognize the separation of individuals, in that whatever arises for them from this sexual interest is external to them and not truly a form of psyche. Even though the external form represents something quite dramatic, the separation of beings provides the safety of assuming that they are not the content of such inner turmoil. This creates a judicial barrier: although the representational material is dramatic, the separation of beings provides the safety of assuming that they are not the content of such inner turmoil. This becomes complex when the dynamic between them is codependent, with no clear boundaries, leading to the assumption that highly nihilistic material is represented by the external form.

External Representations and Psychological Implications

Not all external forms will result in the representation of marginalized internal organic matter. Only those that are directly connected to the organic matter itself, such as sexual interests in the case of sexuality, will trigger this process. Although we have focused on marginalized sexual material, this concept can be applied to any organic matter, depending on the external form that is connected to it. Similarly, this process can also extend to any marginalized aspects of the mind, which might manifest through external forms. While sexuality is inherently organic, other aspects of the psyche that are not initially organic can still become organically coupled. For example, if a trauma that the psyche has marginalized becomes externalized through the experience of another person, an organic component remains involved in this process.

The trauma creates a state in the body that induces new organic expression, leaving an imprint on the biological system that may persist across generations. This newly formed organic matter will be intricately linked with the mental material associated with the trauma.

This resolves the physiological problem that Freud mentioned in the *Pleasure Principle*, where trauma is more acutely experienced when there is no physical effect.[19] Those who do not sustain injury are more exposed to trauma than those who do, as was the case of war veterans. This occurs because the organic structure absorbed the experience under the assumption of a perceptual-related interaction. When that interaction does not occur, it creates a domain for itself within the organic structure, as there was no object for the initial response. Thus, it waits in the background for further elaboration as to why the reaction arose to satisfy an existential experience endured by the psyche. Consequently, deliberation is necessary to explain the situational and circumstantial aspects that caused this biological response to arise.

Without the perceptual interaction, the trauma-induced experience has no facilitating interaction within the external world. It arose to partake in an assumed perception, and when it did not arise, it was left waiting for interaction. The domain within the organic structure will seek to interact, as it feels deserving of the experience. To satisfy that organic element, one would need to interact with the representational material that ascends from that trauma. The same applies to sexuality; to deal with neglected material of the organic structure, one must interact with the sexual representations of the mind and its absolute objective.

Thoughts and Biological Processes

For thoughts can create biological processes, which, even when detached from the thoughts themselves, will express a life of their own. The fear imposed on the body will not only be mentally recollected but will also persist in the core organic structure as a biological entity. When marginalized mental material is not integrated into much of the organic structure, it will not engage the processes we've described. Although it may be necessary for the psyche's organic response and symptoms, there will be no psychological demand. Therefore, the organic matter neglected by the psyche becomes the sole cause for the representation of these nihilistic thoughts and the dramatic external forms that embody them.

The mental imposition of the sexual drive is the fairest way to control it. There is this line of dialogue that transforms the instinct into many different forms, to which the outcome is far different than the initial intention. The cost of such power is that the absolute instinct will create sub-sexual aspects that will be represented in the psyche and will cause both internal and social unrest, as mentioned earlier. However, allowing unrestricted sexual expression and access, devoid of mental scripts and feats of sublimation, might be considered a problematic sexual function. For the absolute sexual tone is one of extreme degrees, containing objectifications and solicitations, and producing very distinct sexual roles.

This is because there is no filter on organic sexual expression, which tends to manifest in an imposing way, without concern for social norms. Only a mental filter applies, which directly causes a gap toward absolute sexuality.

Consider how highly intelligent mammals express sexuality, with a certain sophistication, and we approach the absolute form of sexuality. It seeks what it seeks, without understanding or concern for the process.

Sexual roles become clearly defined because the organic material itself enforces them with such veracity and certainty. These roles are shaped by many factors, ultimately leading to a final, organic sexual expression. In that state, it seeks a very specific sexual object, one that feels more tangible to the organic structure than any mental framework. Since it is perceived as so existent, almost as if the object is a part of the organic structure itself, it is defined as holding the potential to satisfy that drive. This creates a pseudo-obsession with the details of that interest, leading to finite objectification. Therefore, objects must contain roles.

The Balance of Self-Control

There is aggression within absolute sexuality, tied to the act of conquering the object of sexual desire. This aggression is a manifestation of the organic material itself, where the object is nearly seen as a part of oneself, separated only by space. To take what one already possesses, both as an object and not a singularity, creates this form of aggression. This is the absolute organic aspect of sexuality.

Another way to control the sexual drive, aside from sublimation or filtering the sexual material through elaborate mental discourse, is via self-control. There is no logical continuity between the organic drive and this control, as it goes against the entire system. It occurs despite one's will or understanding and, therefore, is not part of the sublimation process. Sexual material is allowed to manifest freely, pursuing its objectives effusively. Self-control halts this process from reaching external action. Since it isn't part of the psyche's logical process, it doesn't diminish the organic material. It acts contrary to selfhood and its contents, without facing retribution. This behavior suggests that self-control is a third-party imposition, akin to the external regulator of perception. Psychologically, it embodies the harshness of early caregivers, brought into the psyche to control the system as they did in the early stages of psychological life.

Self-control, when applied excessively counter to the psyche, will be recognized as an oppressor, no different from an external one. A certain amount of this behavior is tolerated because selfhood is deeply dependent on the environment and is willing to subordinate to it. However, too much would diminish the gravity with which one engages with the psyche's workings. In the face of excessive anti-self-control, the psyche will adopt an arbitrary role, and its processes will no longer be sufficiently engaged. Similarly, actions directed toward external reality, emanating from the psyche, will be seen as pseudo-reality, viewed as arbitrary in relation to self-control. The entire reason that one could contradict selfhood with a mechanism of self-control is an allowance to dominate oneself without abiding by the rule of logic. Since we cannot work through every piece of mental material prior to action, we requisite a mechanism that can override the system.

The benefit of self-control in the sexual process is that, in a certain sense, it demonstrates that absolute sexuality is being represented to such a degree that only a non-logical imposition could prevent it from disrupting social affairs. If one requires something non-mental to manage sexuality, this suggests that sexuality itself is free from mental impositions or sublimation.

Another consideration is that by employing this anti-self-control, the organic material is brought to the forefront through the diminishing of the psyche. In subordinating the psyche, its grip on the representations of the organic material is loosened, allowing the latter to find its natural expression. However, the caveat to this approach is that the demands of anti-self-control oppose every aspect of both the psyche and organic material. In this way, the new oppressor merely weakens the old one and proceeds to dominate the organic material from the level of perception-reality rather than psyche-reality.

Thus, we find a delicate balance: if excessive self-control is exercised in the sexual domain, it elevates the entire psyche as a serious entity; but if mental impositions are applied instead, they introduce a chain of problematic psychological discontinuities. Mental imposition treats the organic material as arbitrary, while self-control treats the psyche as arbitrary.

Sexuality and Climax

Sexuality can be defined at any stage of its climax to fulfill a higher narrative that is seemingly logical in an organism's lifetime. Even as we can view a particular sexual interaction as a concluded enterprise, the orgasm can very well be viewed as a sexual expression among a larger system of climaxes. This individualistic sexual experience is seen as a continuing sexual thought that squares to a certain climactic experience through multiple sexual experiences. Just as it is known to the organism that infantile masturbation or non-climactic sexual experiences are for the betterment of a growing sexual agent (Freud), so is a mature sexual experience to be viewed for its superior offering of sexual knowledge.

This is why the organism is fared to follow a masturbation liability, for in each self-sexual episode, there will be a formation of necessities to perform at a higher advantage in factual sexual interactions. Yet, we must know the limit: for if every sexual interaction is serving a larger sexual narrative, then we must find able ground to settle a certain culmination of sexuality. We need to set a principle of scale to which something would be considered climactic, while others will be considered "foreplay."

A narrative arc can be extended, but is sure to need its dip into the climactic curve towards the destination. We can understand that without adequate foreplay, the sexual experience would not be wholeheartedly climactic. Consequently, there is a requirement of sexual building and another of reconciliation. Without the continued edifice, that is surrendering sexual interaction for the elaboration of absolute sexuality, it would result in declined performance and vitality.

Similar to the ongoing sexuality of a single person, where the beginning holds the advantage of being a climactic experience for the development of sexuality, the later stages will require the same method used prior to sexual relations: a landscape of sexual buildup without a focus on climax. We are obliged to consider the critique against those who assert sexual reproduction as permanently centric, where the implantation of the semen is always the attention. This type of sharpness will produce inadequate sexual forming, which does require a certain availability for removing the climactic focus for allowing sexual disarray and ambiguity, or freedom for sexual exploration.

However, in removing a centric focus, we allow for sexual availability of any kind, even of sexual interactions with sexual agents other than the particular sexual relationship. We must agree that a certain, albeit unstable, centric focus is required, just as an orgasm will always be the surrounding focus for sexual interaction, to either extract or dispense.

The Question of Focus during Sexual Building

The question remains as to what will be the centric focus during the hiatus for sexual building: it must be something that ascribes to rigor and leads to a period of climactic concentration. We must retain the centric focus of sexual reproduction through normal climactic interaction. As we have stated, this will cause a lack of sexual building due to its rigorous nature, having reproduction as its end-product. However, the difference lies in the stages that lead to the production itself, which can be termed sexual construction. Even as the end-product is the centric focus of reproduction, one can explore a sexual-conceptual network which includes all sexual disarray which is possible.

Even though the inevitable sexual performance will be with the same person, the previous conceptual buildup won't be. The practical instance is rigorous and centric-focused, while all the theoretical development is available for exploration. The reason that sexual construction does not require development concluded to the practical instance is because it does not concern itself with raw physicality. Sexual development is conceptual territory, and the externalities that seem to bring its vitality or imagery are also conceptual. The organism itself is already wired with raw sexuality to perform in a practical manner, irrespective of the conceptual buildup. We don't need to enjoin the practical sexual experience that the conceptual realm has conjured, and it may even be detrimental.

The trouble will be that the organism finds itself at the end of the climactic experience wondering if it was necessary to embody and act out the conceptual landscape of sexuality. It acknowledges a lack of production and seems to balance the cost with the seeming necessity of conceptual actualization. Because it knows itself as a simple reproductive organism, which has the practical climactic experience as its focus, there is a sense of betrayal of the conceptual realm for passing beyond its boundaries into the practical instance in which the organism presides.

Yet we have not solved the equation, for without a practical sexual experience, there will be no stimulating effect upon the conceptual realm to expand a horizon into a world it knows nothing about. For this reason, there must be practical instances of sexuality that stimulate the conceptual landscape but do not further its effect as a practicality for full sexual interaction. This is where sensuality becomes a potent idea, as it has the habit of following a practical formation of sexuality, a sight, a sentiment, without leading to a physical manifestation. The sight flows by, the sentiment being one of many, so that these practical instances do not continue as practical but rather enter immediately into the conceptual landscape of inquiry. The sight flows by but is reimagined for the mind; the sentiment is one of many, but the conceptual realm can handle many.

The practical realm of sexuality forebears a sexual horizon which, instead of allowing it to continue in that realm, becomes exiled into the conceptual realm. This is done by removing the components that make it a physical reality, which are the specificity of the occasion and objects, and rather following a more conceptual outlook of the experience. This would have one remove themselves from the occupancy of that stream of consciousness to move towards supplementary or other sexual formations.

Thus, the conceptual realm becomes the source of sexual insight by flowing between physical objects, a movement that pure physicality alone cannot achieve. This is the poetic reference to sensuality, which will create a universal sense for sexual thoughts so as to remove them from the practical realm to be followed without physical consequence. The climax is most dreaded for the sensual experience because it knows that it will be the demise of all sexual development.

This is a perspective of the structure of reality: to understand that the action which manifests in physical reality is not a conceptual notion of any sort. It is pure biological activity of raw materials of nature and does not partake in any psyche or conscious constructs. There is nothing interesting about a physical action because it does not retain the notion of the observer and its interests. We find interest in physical activity not for its raw state but only through our conceptual abridgment to control for the psyche's connection to reality. Just as a child perceives the intercourse of parents as a hostile act, for it is their conceptual outline that gives any formation to the activity at all.

When we glorify action, we are performing a conceptual enlargement of the material that is reflected upon action. However, most glorifications of action are unaware of this nuance and instead assume that the action itself is a specialty of human affairs. The material that is contained within the action is assumed to be the content and not a mirror poetic representation of the substance, as Aristotle attributes the arts as an imitation.[20] We can observe the physical realm as a mode of operations for the aspects of the organism that do not concern psyche or conscious movements. Such that sexual physicality is not a sexual fantasy in any regard. It is not fantastical, nor does it presume a sexual orientation. It is not hostile, nor stimulating, but it is a discharge of biological material alongside other biological entities.

This sentiment is noticed by individuals who are lacking dynamism in their sexuality, and these are the thoughts that would ruminate. Instead of perceiving such individuals as lacking sexuality, we can instead perceive them as truly understanding the physicality of the situation. The same can be said for non-sexual attractions, which if compelled to perceive sexuality, would notice only the physical elements of such.

Only when we enter a conceptual realm pertaining to sexuality can we notice sexuality in reference to the manner we are discussing. Therefore, there is a point that the final act of sexuality, or the physical manifestation, is not a concern of sexual stimulation. In some sense, foreplay is the entire mode of sexuality.

The true practical instance is not formalized by sensuality but is the end-product of its development. The sensual mind understands that absolute practical sexuality cannot be glorified or outspoken because it is the organism at work, as it has been doing for a very long time on an evolutionary scale.[21] We understand this within the language of obscenities, which usually pertains to sexual references. It is an obscenity in its consideration because it highlights the physical manifestation of sexuality as if it is a conceptual aspect. It is obscene to the reality framework, which understands that the physicality of sexuality is not a sexual reference.

By taking the vulnerability of what is to be considered sure biological material and thrusting it back upon the conceptual realm through its communication device of language, it disrupts reality production. Although we define the word obscene as over-stimulating from normal sociality, we must find a better definition. There are many aspects that are overstimulating for sociality but would not be obscene because they do not threaten the reality framework of conceptual versus physical.

A controversial idea would not be obscene but would be a great trouble for sociality; even as the controversial idea does overstimulate and demands an overbearing conceptual procession, it does not obscene the social realm. What is obscene for sociality is when we take what is biological, that stands under the organic structure, and reveal its humility upon the conceptual realm. Negating the sexual premise, this would be the case for any extreme physicality, such as murder, which will be considered obscene just the same. These biological aspects seek to remain as physical as can be, because they are accurately not connected to the conceptual realm. Even as the conceptual realm may reflect upon these physicalities, it is only as a way of formulating a conceptual realm that does not disturb the physical one.

Almost as if foreplay is the sensual and conceptual elaboration prior to the practical instance, and the climactic ending is the practical instance which grounds the conceptual realm into physical space. This grounding is not a very potent aspect of sexuality because the entire elaboration of sexuality is a conceptual production which, in this case, is being lost to physicality. Why glorify the loss of the very model of operations for the process of glorification?

Absolute Physicality and Conceptual Sexuality

Absolute physicality cannot be sexually stimulating because it does not partake in the conceivable notions of psyche moments. Another reason why the immediate loss of sexuality occurs when the climactic experience is completed; until that moment, there is a slight form of conceptual interplay to bring practical sexuality into its production. When the act is completed, or should I say, enacted with wholeness, the conceptual realm is of no use, and the practical realm stands for itself as a non-sexually stimulating experience.

A notion may enter the negotiation that one can invert the sexual premise, where they follow the conceptual realm into the practical one, ignoring the physical station as a locale of distinction. That they would actualize the sexual fantasy in the external realm so as to invert the clause, to have the physical realm re-emerge from its exile. By disrupting the physical isolation, it will find itself betrayed by the psyche and will seek its retribution. The inversion is a sadist act to disrupt the reality framework through sexual deviation, and this will have the internal masochist, known as the raw biological state, to find itself from the disarray. Like how the discharge is thoroughly ignored during foreplay, and when taking center focus, we leave the confines of foreplay altogether.

An individual can then follow a regimen of multiple sexual interactions that complete the conceptual realm but do so without consequence to the physical one. We must differentiate the foreplay that is devoid of discharge and the discharge that is devoid of physicality. Foreplay does not neglect the discharge, for it does not have the possibility of discharge while remaining foreplay. The period of discharge is the neglect of physical manifestation of the discharge for the conceptual one. Obviously, the performance will eventually lead to a physical manifestation, but that is a byproduct of the intentional experience of the interaction. Differing from foreplay, which avoids the discharge so as to produce the wanting effect of leading to the discharge, when there is no physicality at the point of discharge, there will not arise a new form of post-climax.

For this, it would seem that the organism finds a betrayal in the order of succession, being a loss of physicality, not an enticement for more. By finding itself at a climax without a manifestation, it will accept an existential loss and retreat into itself. This proves problematic for further sexual activity since it requires a certain raw physicality to generate sexual expansion for the conceptual realm. Therefore, the loss of physicality is a true loss, which will not be reattributed in the near future. What is required of the next sexual instance is a more elaborate conceptual portrayal that permeates more material, for it has a greater time accessing the physical strands that have been demoted.

We have partitioned two primary aspects to be enjoined together for a proper sexual manifestation: the first is a conceptual elaboration; the second is physicality in its raw nature. When the continuous sexual relationship lacks stimulation, it is usually because there is a deficient conceptual horizon, as is natural in the instance preceding the relationship. It is not the continuous physicality of that specific person which causes the effect, but the diminution to a conceptual framework that encompasses the full scope of sexuality, as would be during the onset of the relationship.

The specificity of the person may appear to portray a particular conceptual framework, but this is merely an illusion. What this specificity represents are aspects of a sexual conceptual framework that does not originate with the person of interest. The variety of sexual objects is not the point; rather, the objects themselves embody aspects of sexuality. The variation, in turn, serves as an overall sexual representation of dynamic sophistication. The specificity which hosts that sentiment is not the ground for which this is the cause, and one could swiftly move between specificity as long as the elaborated sexual theme remains.

Sexuality and Physicality

A portrayal of a lack of physicality emerges when an elaborate conceptual framework is pursued with such persistence that the organic component is unable to fulfill its role in producing the final outcome. This would result in a belated discharge. The transfer from the conceptual fantasy to the physical organism did not occur, which leads to a conceptual discharge with a physical spillover in the aftermath. At every sexual interaction, there is a point where there is a need to transfer from the fantastical realm, even as it promises more depth and exposure, to the physical organic state taking hold against the conceptual expansion, to eventually see its full demise with the organic matter filling the gap. This we will call the transition period.

A form of sexuality presented as an elaborate visual narrative serves as a conceptual portrayal, inviting the viewer to elaborate their own scheme of sexuality. The transfer from the viewing experience into the physical one, especially in the case of masturbation, may not be effective. Because the conceptual offering is so effective, fulfilling dramatic themes that can far surpass a solitary imaginative instance, it becomes quite difficult to detract from its material and fall into the organic form. The transition period necessitates a process of differentiation, in which a conceptual overload would cause the climax to be mostly conceptual.

For the fall into physicality to be effective, it must not leave over a stark representation of the conceptual realm. A conceptual sexual realm that is too activated from the starting point will automatically imprint into the stage of physicality without differentiation. The physical realm is activated with great desire when the conceptual realm is forthright and thorough; however, upon the entrance and climax of the physical realm, it does not need nor require a conceptual database. It is a fairly competent system of the organism that can provide adequate reproduction and sexual necessities without any psyche involvement. Hence, just like absolute action is devoid of the conceptual realm, absolute sexuality is not a psyche investment.

The Transition Period in Sexuality

We may wonder whether human creation is merely an organic activity, and rightly conclude, from the standpoint of human existentialism, that it is a sophisticated organism functioning independently of the psyche. We may think that a conceptual inference into the genetic code would produce more conceptual and elaborate agents, but that would be like saying that creating a computational device is more sophisticated than a human. In the reflection of the specific conceptual footprint, the genome will be enlarged, but that would be at the expense of the universal hominoid, which does not fit into that mindset.

The organic intention includes the wholeness of the human, encompassing its psychic matter. However, the integration of one's conceptual or conscious development depends on how well it has previously adapted to the sexual climax. It will not be visible in the mental transcode of the individuals partaking in an organic manifestation, but it will be included as long as it has been integrated into the substructure of personhood. Whatever remains merely ruminating on the surface will not be included in the genetic transfer.

It is difficult to pinpoint the moment it would be best to commence the transition because there is always the possibility that a more stimulating aspect will find its way. However, if the onset is chosen too late, there will be too much conceptual material as soon as the climax occurs, and it will be at a loss to the true physical form.

We understand this theme in many other aspects of life, from theory to practice, from game to real life, from fantasy to reality. In each of these arenas, it would be agreed upon that there must be a transition period between the two realms. With the risk of too much theory and insufficient practical application, or too much practical application and too little theory, the game encroaches on aspects that deserve to be respected as real, or an overbearing urgency takes over when the lightness of a game is needed. Fantasy that limits reality, or reality that lacks imaginative sophistication.

In each of these scenarios, it is understandable that both mediums are necessary and deserving of unique and devoted attention. If the fantasy still retains too much realistic rhetoric, then it loses its domain-specific parameter, while if reality retains fantastical elements, then it will find illusionary aspects that would not fulfill reality's demands. Keeping note of the fact that every realm will include the other for certain functionality, fantasy that loses the bearing of certain reality guidelines finds an unrelatable characteristic.

Therefore, each is domain-specific, and in the case of sexuality during the conceptual elaboration, it should be noted to distance from absolute physical manifestation. In fact, we find an immediate decline of sensuality when the mind wanders into fantasy related to physical fulfillment. While during the physical manifestation of the climax of sexuality, it is deserving to be removed from the conceptual fantasy, as it would dampen the organism's machinery from its process of work.

The transition period is thus necessary from the conceptual to the physical realm. Let us examine the details of the transitions between the examples mentioned, between theory and practice, game and real life, and fantasy and reality, as these may transition in a manner similar to sexuality. Since sexuality has psyche and non-psyche components to its structure, it does not have the ability to seamlessly transfer from one to the other and, as such, must involve a dramatic, illogical shift between realms. For example, theory to practice, this current study is theory, and the practical would be how you manifest this information in your dynamic life, which cannot be transitioned by simply asserting, "I have found this idea; let's implement it." This is because there is no congruence with what is mentioned and the detailed complexity of practical life.

Application can be a result of theory but does not comprise logical consistency between them. It appears logical when it is laid out in an objective forum, but the practical realm is physical and embodied with the five senses. Theory can be a major influence on practicality, but the attempt to apply theory directly to practice is a road that loses true practicality. True practicality is the ability for the wholeness of everything to be affected.

Fantasy and reality undergo the same kind of shift: if not properly differentiated, the fantasy elements become absorbed into the reality framework, just as theory begins to enter the practical realm, treating the world almost like a mathematical equation. Because the transition is so immediate, there is no existential gap allowing the true transfer of material into a new dimension.

Fundamental Purpose

It's important to note that for all sexual unions, there is a prerequisite for the dynamic to have a third-party element. This is the *fundamental purpose* of joining forces, the reason each partner seeks the union. For a friendship to be considered dynamic, each party must have a clear vision of why they are friends. When the reason for the friendship dissipates, for instance, when they depart an institution, and no other reason replaces it, the friendship will weaken. Usually, all dynamics involve a third party that is perceptually vibrant; it might be an institution, a collective, an identity, or familial attachments. This pertains to less intimate dynamic relationships that require a preconceived formulation for the participants. Each party engages under the dominion of that fundamental purpose, and all developments in dynamic learning relate to that purpose.

A friendship grounded in the fundamental purpose of existing as neighbors will engage in a dynamic related to neighboring. This will involve the entire family, which will affect the friendship since that is the fundamental purpose. The friendship will mirror the parental relationships in addition to the neighboring sentiment. When there is conflict in the neighborhood, it will manifest correspondingly in the friendship. The friendship can replace the fundamental purpose, especially when tested regarding the neighboring dynamic. They may find another fundamental purpose, such as a common interest, or it might become more intimate by emerging each other's character. The fundamental purpose of exploring each other's emotional development will be tested when one party withholds information, threatening that novel purpose.

Now that we've explored the concept of fundamental purpose in relationships, let's understand this concept in regard to intimate interactions. When the dynamic becomes more intimate, the fundamental purpose must be more elaborate and realistic. An institution would not preserve the fundamental purpose as per engaging in an intimate dynamic since the binding element is a "worldly construct."

Institutions do not exist in the biological state of a social beings; they exist as intellectual fabrications. However, upon closer examination of intellectual constructs, it becomes evident that institutions are inherently worldly rather than intimate, just like any intellectual formulation. The intimate dimensions pertain to the natural components of selfhood, which are not constructed or proposed nonetheless, exist as they are. Worldly notions are a form of learning, although they do not remain under biological pressure. Intellectual or social constructs, although serving the expansive awareness of intimacy (as this work attempts to prepare), cannot be the fundamental purpose for sexual intimacy.

The Role of the Body in Sexual Dynamics

The fundamental purpose of the relationship will replicate itself throughout, as the initial seed replicates itself throughout the social structure. By nature, the institution lacks an intimate dimension and cannot foster a truly intimate dynamic within its sphere. The fundamental purpose determines the level of intimacy in any dynamic and, based on its constitution, the ability to contain a sexual dynamic.

A sexual dynamic is automatically intimate because of the individual's association to their biological body. The body is not a construct which mind assumes; rather, intimacy is a construct of the experience of the body. The body is the organism that contains one's experience of existence, and every component of selfhood is connected to the body as such. The body is the gathering point of connection; all other connections are merely similarities to the rudimentary experience of the body.

Engaging one's body with another's allows a person to explore and mirror their own bodily connection. When an individual seeks the "intimate" parts of a sexual partner, they are essentially mapping their own intimate areas. The exploration during a sexual union serves both to understand the biological body they experience within themselves and to discover pleasure that cannot be found through their own bodily connection alone, by eliciting pleasure in another, they stimulate hidden pleasure within their own body.

Disconnection from the Body

We may ask how an individual can become disconnected from their own body. This disconnection arises from the very structure of life itself. To engage with the external world, we must, by necessity, withdraw from the immediacy of bodily experience. Without that detachment, it would be impossible to center on anything beyond the self. But once we leave the domain of the body, we cannot simply return, the connection is disrupted, and the path back is obscured.

In neglecting the body, we perform a psychological leap into another domain, one that does not allow a natural or intuitive return. There is no rational reason to sever this connection; whatever enables such neglect is neither natural nor logical. Once the mind shifts away, it no longer intuits the body. It becomes absorbed in a realm beyond the body, where its logic no longer applies to bodily experience. Thus, returning to the body is not a matter of reason or will, it is a return to a domain which the mind no longer inhabits.

No buried memory or subconscious material can fully restore this connection. The way back lies through sexuality, which engages imagination, identity, social constructs, and sexual scripts, intellectual frameworks that can guide, indirectly, back toward the body. These external elements must be integrated into selfhood, allowing the body to rediscover its peculiar path back to itself.

The External Body and Sexuality

The sexual partner is an external body most resembling the biological nature of selfhood but nevertheless has external characteristics. If that sexual body weren't external, it wouldn't allow access to one's own body since the internal system has completely neglected it. The external body benefits from being external while also existing as a humanoid body much like one's own. Intellectual domains, such as social constructs, provide the material that makes the union of two sexual bodies worthwhile. Without this intellectual layer, the union lacks an external framework to anchor itself, making it more likely to hinder connection than to cultivate it.

The reason the body is conventionally of the opposite gender is that the intellectual construct uses the organism's need for integration. Sexual scripts vary, but at their core, they involve integration and disintegration. The male-to-female narrative fits the sexual script in a satisfactory manner because the integration is physically transparent. The faintness of conventional genders is that, although sexual response is heightened, the opposing gender lacks similarity, which hinders connection to one's own body.

Connection to one's body through the opposite gender occurs by recognizing the parts of their body deficient in their partner. This recognition produces shame of their own body's vulnerability. This shame commences the connection to their own body, forcing them to confront this "broken figure." The shame results from a willingness to copiously connect to their body, which, upon seeing what is lacking, recognizes what is present.

Substantially, two bodies of the same gender engage more directly in connecting to their private bodies. The same-gender experience of their identifiable bodies is very direct; without shame as a medium, they perceive what they contain. They attach quickly and integrate the notion of their body into their persona more rapidly. They gain more intuitive knowledge of their body but mislay the dynamic scripts of intellectual constructs. This is not to say there is no script, but it is less "natural" than the conventional form of sexuality. Same-sex dynamics advance in bodily connection at the expense of intellectual constructs, while heterosexual dynamics gain in intellectual constructs at the expense of bodily connection.

Heterosexuality is susceptible by the simplistic tone of non-heterosexuals' connection to their body. They desire that heightened experience, even at the expense of weakened sexual scripts. Understanding intimacy and intervals allows heterosexual dynamics to reach bodily connection and realize the non-heterosexual offering as non-threatening. The intimidation arises from the unwillingness to lose intellectual gains or to undertake the work of understanding intimacy and intervals, necessary to experience their bodies similarly to non-heterosexual individuals. The intimidation is perceived as losing status quo, becoming non-heterosexual, or developing their sexual domain tenfold.

Identity and Sexual Dynamics

An identity, when used as the fundamental purpose of a relationship, cannot contain or sustain a sexual dynamic because identity, by its nature, does not offer true intimacy. While identity is more intimate than an institution, since it is carried as a perceived extension of the self, it remains a social construct. Identity tends to persist across daily interactions, whereas institutions are rooted in external structures like location and formal arrangements. Marriage, for instance, is an institution, not an identity, as it is a structured formulation of a relationship. Identity may participate in marriage to lend it a sense of intimacy, but it does not define or sustain it.

Though identity plays a crucial role in self-perception, it is insufficient as the core of an intimate union. For a sexual dynamic to be truly intimate and enduring, there must be something inherent within both individuals, something deeper than institutional or social definitions, which serves as the fundamental purpose. Institutions and identities, while evocative, fall short of encompassing the deeply personal and embodied dimensions required for authentic sexual intimacy.

The Inherent Foundational Purpose for Sexual Intimacy

The fundamental purpose of sexual intimacy must reflect the depth of intimacy it seeks to sustain. It must arise from something inherent within both partners, something that exists apart from society. Even exclusive common ground is insufficient for true intimacy if it can still be found elsewhere; it lacks the intrinsic uniqueness that defines a deeply personal connection.

When we view one describe their love, they usually suggest a distinct, personal notion of love in the other person. Love, in this sense, can be understood as a heightened form of pleasure. We begin with liking, an experience closely tied to pleasure, and gradually move toward love, which is simply a more intense, enduring version of that same pleasure. For a sexual union to be genuinely intimate, its fundamental purpose must be a shared experience of pleasure that is unique to the couple, deeply personal, psychologically impactful, and imperceptible to anyone outside the relationship.

One might assume that friendship is sustained by an intimate, shared pleasure without the need for a separate fundamental purpose. But this assumption falters when one person relocates and the friendship fades. If the relationship were truly grounded with internal pleasure, external circumstances like lifestyle changes wouldn't dissolve it. While friendships may occasionally draw on intimate internal elements, they are typically supported by other, more situational fundamental purposes.

A truly intimate dynamic endures regardless of changes in environment or circumstance because its fundamental purpose is internal, never externalized, and always takes precedence over the external realm. This internal purpose functions like the institutional basis that underpins and legitimizes friendships, acting as a mediator of the relationship itself. Just as friendships weaken when the institution that sustains them changes, intimate dynamics weaken when their pleasure-based purpose, whether sexual or relational, dissipates.

We might assume friendship uses an intimate common pleasure without relying on another fundamental purpose. Yet, this is not the case, if for instance, one moves to a new location deprived of friends continuing with them. If the fundamental purpose were a dynamic pleasure, they would not lose the relationship due to lifestyle changes. Even if friendship occasionally uses an intimate seed, it relies on other fundamental purposes.

A truly intimate dynamic would persist despite location or lifestyle changes. The fundamental purpose is internal, never externalized, and always a priority over external environments. This fundamental purpose resembles the institution that grants friendships and mediates relationships. When the fundamental purpose, sexual or dynamic, dissipates, just as when changing institutions modifies friendships, the intimate dynamic weakens.

The Centrality of Pleasure in Sexual Intimacy

As stated, the fundamental purpose of intimacy is pleasure. As long as it exists for both parties, the dynamic continues, specifically regarding sexual pleasure. Less intimate components require a less intimate *fundamental purpose*. An intimate dynamic lacking a sophisticated identity also is short of a fundamental purpose; however, this impends the institution of the relationship, not the sexual dynamic. Couples may engage intimate sexual interactions yet dissociate due to lack of institutional support.

Conversely, couples who share an institutional identity but lack sexual fulfillment will inevitably weaken over time. The true fundamental purpose of an intimate relationship is sexual pleasure. Without it, the relationship cannot even be considered a friendship. Because intimacy is rooted in sexuality, attempting to perform intimacy without a sexual component undermines the very foundation of the relationship. If both partners experience a diminished libido, mutually agreeing to abstain from sexual intimacy, the relationship will naturally deteriorate. Sexual intimacy is not a byproduct of intimacy; rather, intimacy originates from sexual connection.

Intimacy is inherently connected to the body. When intimacy is expressed without physical interaction, it treats intimacy as something detached from bodily union. The reason such unified lifestyles exist within intimate relationships, living together, sharing expenses, raising children, is because they are grounded in intimacy. These behaviors do not occur among ordinary friends because regular friendships do not contain bodily intimacy that underpins such commitment. Intimacy is the central purpose of the entire relationship; all other elements are secondary structures that support it.

We can easily imagine open marriages, sexual relationships without marriage, or friendships without a sexual component. However, we cannot truly conceive of an intimate relationship that lacks sexual intimacy. A marriage without sex or "intimate friends" who are not sexually active would more accurately be described as "close friends." The demands of a shared life, cohabitation, financial interdependence, parenting, relocation, and discussions of romantic or sexual partners, are exclusive to intimate relationships, which are defined by their sexual foundation. While a sexual relationship can exist without these relational responsibilities, the reverse is not true: a relationship that takes on these responsibilities deprived of sexual intimacy lacks the core of intimacy itself.

A sexually intimate relationship requires a multi-layered foundation: a fundamental purpose for the intimacy itself, a basis for relational structure, and an institutional framework, such as marriage, that helps sustain the non-intimate aspect of partnership. The institution of marriage exists to preserve the union through periods of strain or when other foundational purposes deteriorate. Finally, such a relationship would also include a shared identity, allowing for rituals, a sense of commonality, and the maintenance of a familial or communal structure.

External Factors of a Sexual Union

When a sexual union occurs owed to a less intimate fundamental purpose, the union lacks sophistication and genuine pleasure, for the reason that pleasure is not the central purpose. Instead, it relies on simplistic external factors to justify the connection. For example, if two people come together because they share a collective identity, that identity can become the primary purpose of their sexual union. Even if the collective identity promotes a sensual lifestyle, using it as the fundamental purpose removes true pleasure from the experience. While they may still experience sexual pleasure, it is not the primary force. We can test this by removing the environmental purpose, the identity, and observing whether the sexual dynamic thrives. Alternatively, we can gauge this by having them seek more intimacy and noticing resistance, which indicates that pleasure was not the fundamental purpose.

This also occurs when less intimate drives, from other areas of the relationship, spill over into the sexual dynamic. These less intimate purposes are not confined to their original domains and can take hold of the sexual connection. While they may help the relationship thrive in a general sense, they act as a deterrent to more intimate forms of connection. For instance, if a relationship is rooted in an identity or community, that identity can become the fundamental purpose for sexual intimacy. If the community holds certain ideological views about sexuality, those views may outline the couple's sexual dynamics, overshadowing true intimacy.

Consider a couple whose friendship is based on an institution. If they use that institution as the fundamental purpose for their sexual relationship, they are not exploring intimacy beyond it. When institutional work takes precedence over the sexual union, it becomes the central purpose. In such cases, the couple might discuss private sexual matters at the institution, whether cynically, sarcastically, subconsciously, or seriously, because their sexual intimacy is governed by the same fundamental purpose that drives their institutional life. Having the institution as a third-party influence requires addressing intimacy within that domain specifically.

The Role of a Third-party in Sexual Dynamics

Consider a couple seeking therapy to improve their sexual intimacy. In doing so, they effectively elevate the therapist to the central purpose of their sexual union. Before involving this third party, their relationship was driven by other core purposes. Once the therapist enters the picture, they become part of the couple's intimate space and begin to outline its trajectory.

In much the same way, when a third party is introduced into a two-person sexual union, that person becomes the central reference point for intimacy. Their presence reorients the dynamic, not only influencing the relationship but also becoming its new focus. During sexual activity, the original pair engages with each other through the third party, who acts as an intermediary and defines the evolving structure of interaction. While roles may shift throughout, the third party remains an essential presence.

This third participant effectively becomes the recipient of pleasure, replacing what, in a dyad, exists as a shared, intangible experience. In a duo, pleasure is distributed and co-created; something between the two, not wholly belonging to either. In a threesome, the third party becomes the embodiment of pleasure itself. Rather than existing between participants, pleasure is consolidated into the third person. After climax, the original pair often finds their pleasure diminished, while the third person becomes burdened with the emotional and physical weight of gratification.

One of the main drawbacks of this arrangement is that the two non-central participants do not engage in developmental learning from the dynamic. They only mirror the third party's pleasure, lacking intrinsic pleasure. Unlike a duo, where one may be the "pleasure partner" at differing times, in a triadic dynamic, the third party is not simply a shifting participant in the pleasure dynamic but becomes the complete embodiment of pleasure itself. The third party does not experience pleasure in the same sense as a masochist, who derives it from a duo dynamic. Instead, the third-party experience is one of *embodied pleasure*, not *invoked pleasure*. The difference between the two is that embodied pleasure does not allow for active participation, while invoked pleasure is entirely active.

We can understand this by comparing the distinguishing elements of invoked pleasure and embodied pleasure. The pleasure one experiences from immediate gratification enters the psyche without the necessary cognitive framework to fully process it. It resembles the way children experience pleasure: raw, immersive, and lacking reflective understanding. This kind of "childlike pleasure" is comparable to the effect of ingesting psychoactive substances, which instantaneously alter experience.

Alcohol, for instance, is commonly associated with immediate gratification due to its quick alteration of both mental and physical states; chemical ingestion altering the biological process of experience. The immediacy of alcohol's effect on the physical and mental arenas has earned it the marker of immediate gratification.

Yet, claiming that the mere use of a pleasure-substance is inherently immediate is only partially correct. The substance changes the experience of the psyche in a moment, however, any perceptual material, such as traumatic exposure, can also affect the psyche, arguably faster than alcohol. Therefore, we cannot confine any stimulus or substance to be inherently a source of *immediate* gratification. The immediacy attributed to a substance results from its common usage as a quick means of gratification.

Invoked Versus Embodied Pleasure

To distinguish 'invoked pleasure' from embodied pleasure, we can conceptualize alcohol as an example of invoked pleasure. Typically, alcohol represents an embodied pleasure, but this can change depending on the approach taken toward the substance. For example, if we engage in ritualistic preparation or designate a special occasion for alcohol consumption, the experience may shift to become an invocation of pleasure. The immediate biological effect of alcohol does not negate this shift, as the preconceived frameworks allow alcohol to serve a distinct purpose. The special occasion then becomes the fundamental reason for consuming the alcohol, accompanied by mental preparation, both in terms of time and depth. In this context, alcohol invokes the pleasure of the occasion and serves as a medium for the entire, profound experience.

In contrast, when substance abuse is involved, the substance takes the role of embodied pleasure. Here, there is no preconceived, fundamental purpose for its use. Instead, the consumption of alcohol becomes defined by its active, subjective role, which 'houses' the act of drinking.

Similarly, in a threesome sexual union, the pleasure experienced by the two participants as they mirror the third participant can be understood as 'embodied pleasure.' In this case, whatever the third participant experiences becomes the pleasure of the other two members, while the third individual lacks active participation in the pleasure. Both the two participants and the third-party fail to actively engage in the pleasure because it is too complete to allow for human interaction. The fantasy of a threesome often reflects the belief that it represents the ultimate form of pleasure in a sexual union, something that a duo cannot achieve. Much like the appeal of alcohol as a gratifying substance, the pleasure gained in this context feels more complete than what is achieved through natural means. However, this completeness is also its flaw, as it leaves no room for individual participation.

As a result, the participants depart from the experience with diminished opportunities for gendered and character-based learning, as well as a sense of drifting pleasure. The threesome represents the 'potential' of pleasure within a sexual union, but when physically enacted, it remains a potentiality for everyone except the third participant. By simply engaging in the act, the dynamic shifts away from invoking pleasure and instead becomes embodied pleasure, which is not adequately received. True potential cannot be fully realized; the closer one gets to it, the less it can be called potential.

Secondly, in a threesome, the third party becomes the fundamental purpose of the entire dynamic. When the fundamental purpose is embodied by a person, it automatically weakens the state of pleasure between the participants, as it relies on an external factor rather than an internal connection. This is similar to when a therapist becomes the central purpose of therapy, externalizing what is inherently an intimate, internal matter. In therapy, individuals still seek to address personal matters within the confines of the therapist's office, hoping that their intimacy will thrive through the process. However, when an external mediation becomes the central purpose of a relationship, separation from that mediator leads to the dissolution of the union's pleasure. The hope of such a dynamic is that the couple will strengthen their union to the point where pleasure becomes intrinsic to their relationship, making it difficult for the therapist, or any external party, to interfere with that intimate bond.

External Influence in Intimate Relationships

This also applies to all elements of an intimate relationship, even those not related to sexuality. When allowing a third-party into a relationship's privacy, they become the fundamental purpose for the union. Cult leaders, for instance, often exploit this dynamic, encouraging people to confide every intimate detail of their relationships, thus binding the relationship to the leader. This is a mechanism of control, even over the most personal matters, achieved simply by having the individuals reveal the details of their intimacy. As Shakespeare put it, "love that is told ceases to be," which encapsulates this phenomenon. By making someone privy to the intimate aspects of love, they become the reason for the relationship, and the relationship, now a public matter, loses its private, intimate essence.[22]

This concept can be applied to any setting. For example, an institution relies on a core purpose that sustains its success. This purpose is what drives the institution's existence, but when it is subject to discussion or scrutiny, the institution may falter or be forced to adopt a new vision. The discussion might seem to enrich the institution, providing depth and insight, but what's really happening is that those engaging in the discussion are becoming the new central purpose of the institution's actuality.

To understand this more clearly, imagine a street or store sign, which informs passersby about what exists at a particular location. When there is a discussion about the sign, the focus shifts from the location itself to the question of its existence. During this discussion, the fate of the location is effectively in the hands of those questioning it. Similarly, when an institution's vision is questioned, it temporarily falls under the control of those who engage in the debate. In essence, the very foundation of the institution rests on its core purpose, by questioning that purpose, the institution loses its stability. During this questioning phase, the institution is in the hands of those involved in the discussion.

This dynamic can also apply to intimate relationships, anyone can question and attempt to govern a relationship, but only if both parties agree to or participate in the dialogue. If they are indifferent or defensive toward such discussions, they only strengthen their own private reasons for maintaining the relationship, contrasting with the external pressures of society.

Characteristic of Sexuality

The Nature of Sexual Interplay: Gender, Distance, and Desire

Sexuality depends on the interplay of genders, and the more distinct the gendered attributes of the participating parties, the more definite sexuality becomes. Interplay is an illustration of the nature of sexuality, which requires two elements: 'inter' and 'play'. The 'inter' aspect is the engagement of two parties in an intersecting manner which, if we are to understand the nature of sexuality as the most intimate, this would be the most intimate intersection.

The second aspect, 'play', is incumbent on normal sexuality, which has the participating members playfully engaging in the union. The engagement is balanced and consequently it does not take on the absolute form of pure reproduction or representation of existential figures. The decline of a sexual instinct arises when the perception of the human body is the human body as its raw form, focused on its organizational system as it appears in the present moment. It stands as a cluster of existence without a glimmer of sensation toward its naturalistic form. While the notion of play would elicit a demand of each party to participate, enticed by the organic nature of self-sufficiency through various physical and conceptual gains produced from such an intersection.

Conceptual Frameworks and the Role of Play in Sexual Engagement

The matter of engaging in pseudo-reality is meant to distract from the purely biological elements, accordingly, an arrangement of intimacy is somewhat objective. This play, in the form of objective intersection, which is not entertained as an absolute reality, harnesses the supremacy of levels of engagement which are not available in the absolute sense. The extraction of interaction absent from its biological form creates the groundwork for interpretation and experience. The play makes one feel as if they are a third-party who oversees the experience and could make use of many dimensions, all which will award an expansive view of that intersection.

Part Two: Sexuality

In some sense, this relaxes the two parties to be as distant as possible so that the intersection is as expansive as presented. If there is an absolute sense to the intersection, then there is no distance between the parties, akin to a domain that is quite restricted by the inability to experience diverse views.

The distance is created when the notion of intersection is a form of play in which it does not portray a representation to a more realistic sense of experience. This allows the spatial distance between the absolute situational plateau and the *game* which has been constructed to be broader than life, in which it now becomes available for an expansive intersection.

When two points on a linear path are close together, their interaction only affects the material directly between them. However, when the points are farther apart, their interaction encompasses a wider range of points along the way, resulting in a composite effect from all the elements in between.

This can be likened to the fantasy of group-sex, which often appeals to many as an amplified sexual desire. The idea of a group introduces multiple potential interactions leading to a final intersection, this culmination of availability and possibility. The key difference is that group-sex plays out in a real-world context, with each participant representing a variation along the sexual spectrum. In contrast, this is a manifestation of internal sexuality, where, even though the ultimate interaction in any sexual encounter involves only two people, the diversity of potential experiences in the space between those two points offers a range of possibilities and dynamics.

Therefore, the first encounter of sexual intersection is usually a fairly intimate and highly active occasion. Because the two parties have arrived from the expanse alongside all of their separate and personal affairs, the occurring intersection has a fair distance between them. In some sense, this would be the ultimate pleasure, in which the relation to absolute biological interaction and its conceptual paradigm is quite distant. The parties involved are engaging in a game where all points along the line are considered, not limited by the typical reproductive context of their interaction. Instead, the focus is on the diverse spectrum of experiences and dynamics, beyond just the final outcome. On the opposite extreme, when sexuality is so detached from reproduction or any natural biological context, its pleasure may diminish. This occurs because the conceptualization becomes too abstract or disconnected, making it difficult for the interaction to align with the inherent, existential nature of sexual experience.

Critical Sexual Theory

Biology, Reproduction, and the Evolution of Sexual Pleasure

Another sexual situation comes to mind: one of strangers instantaneously engaging in sexual intersection, creating total distance, which, on the surface, might seem to promise a more intensified form of sexuality. Nevertheless, the distance remains, as with any organism on the evolutionary chain. A non-anthropomorphic sexual object, devoid of human-like qualities that reflect validation, would be the most distant and thus the most diverse from human experience. Because it cannot existentially intersect in a way that aligns with reproduction or effective receptivity, it fails to provide absolute sexual pleasure.

This added notion of the reception in adequate measure is an important criterion to sexual affectation. When both parties do not participate in the conceptual game of sexuality with equal commitment, the structure of its reality becomes fragile, and so does the experience of the interaction and intersection. Just like in any game where one player is not fully engaged, the experience for all participants within the reality framework is weakened.

We will discuss the inevitable decline of libido when such fantasies are repeatedly enacted. For now, however, we focus on the fantastic nature of certain sexual interests, which reveal the spatial distance at play in the intersection. A married couple, following a conflict, on vacation, in a new environment, during a transitional phase, a holiday, or similar occasions, all of these scenarios heighten sexuality when there is a significant distance between the parties involved in the intersection.

One of the reasons that social language becomes cryptic in reference to sexuality is because direct language will be the call for an absolute sense of it. Any noted reference is usually not directed to the reality of the interaction, and when entertained from that perspective, it is found to be uneventful.

When the engagement occurs in which either of the parties are not participating at the level of 'play,' then the interaction is expending devices of intimacy with non-intimate conceptual frameworks. This can occur both in the zealousness of 'play,' which causes the game to be taken too seriously, or for being apathetic to the game at all. The notion of 'play' carries an intricate balance of these two extremes.

The roles of play are part of the package of the game and when that representation is questioned, so is the game. For instance, masculine and feminine roles play a crucial part in the responsiveness of the game, even if we could conceptually dismiss their legitimacy. Other roles are also necessary within the constructed reality framework, ensuring that all participants are considered active players during the interaction. The legitimacy of these roles is granted by the reality framework itself, which dictates that certain types of games require specific roles tied to them. The reason masculine and feminine roles are so effective in their historical context is that their intersection is intrinsically linked to the organic interaction of reproduction. By fulfilling a role that both aligns with the existential nature of the interaction and the conceptual framework built around it, these roles promise a heightened sexual pleasure.

Even when the sexual interaction has no way of performing the biological product of sexuality, it will borrow from those biological aspects to stimulate a firm ground, allowing the broader conceptual game to overlay upon that stimulus. Thus, we will find the notion of 'teaching' to be a same-sex conceptual framework, which will satisfy the biological layer that will become more adept to overall sexuality in the benefit of this interaction. The performance of biological sexuality, therefore, can always be refined, leading to a more fulfilling product.

The conceptual game built upon this could aim to teach ideas that are both stimulating and intellectually enriching. In this structure, the roles of each party, teacher or student, ultimately connect back to their biological foundations, as discussed earlier. Another layer of biological grounding is the validation of masculine or feminine dispositions. In this way, biology serves to create more defined roles for each gender, ensuring that sexual performance of the future will be more successful. This does not disrupt the depth of the sexual game that is played upon that, which could be the advantageous intersection of masculine and feminine aspects that often fail in normative exchanges.

Shame, too, is a biological foundation for sexual interactions, as it fosters self-awareness and self-consciousness for the fragmented parts of the psyche. This self-awareness is a very potent promise to the biological department for eventual procreation. The awareness of selfhood will grant selfhood's most primary clause of reproducing the organic structure. The spotlight on oneself naturally amplifies reproductive sensitivities. The role for the sexual proponents is of shame in their innocence and guilt. Even without any other aspect of reproduction, shame itself would be considered a reproductive byproduct.

Therefore, any being who engages in a reality framework, where there is an agreement and commitment to its structure, and where the roles of innocence and guilt are embodied, will be capable of stimulation, even in the absence of sex. Accordingly, there is no clear criteria for normative sexuality. The self-conscious experience that will arise from an innocent-guilty interface will be short-lived because it is only based on the expectation of the reproductive encounters that will manifest. When reproduction does not materialize, one is driven to delve deeper into more complex themes of innocence and guilt, which promise heightened self-consciousness and, in turn, greater reproductive potential.

When this persists without reproduction, one must shift to a new mode of sexuality that promises reproduction through an alternative method. Thus, the difference between heterosexuality and non-normative sexuality in this context is that the game must shift at a much faster pace than in heterosexuality. This does not grant amnesty to the hetero, as the reproduction department does not equate all effective reproduction to be the same. It is not content with continuous reproduction lacking diversity within the system that reproduces. Diversity offers a more promising form of reproduction, one that advances the genes toward an immortal future.

Therefore, if the game of sexuality remains the same, it will merely reflect similar gene structures in different human bodies, yet be deemed unprepared for immortality. As with non-normative sexuality that must transition between games to find biological justification, the hetero interaction must move between games so as to find personal diversity in all its fragments and potentials. Immortality is its only absolute focus, so that the path toward it must be both personal diversity and biological ground.

When this does not seem probable for the promising sexual interaction, the sexual pleasure and stimulation will decline exponentially. Thus, the individual who stands at the intersection of a variety of sexual interactions, with a diverse set of games to preserve their continuing nature, will stumble upon the realization that they will begin to be stimulated only by a single individual. This is because biological grounding has become such a necessity that it will disrupt all sexual flow until it follows a reproductive path that requires the continual attention of a single game and subsequent individual.

Part Two: Sexuality

There are necessary characteristics that each proponent must possess for the sexual intersection to work. The genders involved in a sexual union embody specific characteristics that each party upholds for the specific dynamic. These genders are not general to the entire lifestyle of the individual; they relate only to this specific union of time and place.

This is because one can hold a single characteristic while the entirety of the individual transcends it, creating a conceptual overlay. For the intersection to be considered fair, both parties must retain opposing characteristics to ensure a true interplay. The heightened form of sexuality would thus be when the characteristics of each side are as different from each other as possible, with the union being a sure experience of interplay.

The experience of sexuality is shared; instead of having two opposites engage for their own objectives, they maintain a common interest contained by the sexual union. This is contrary to the opposing characteristics which, in any other engagement, would not seek such a partnership. But with intimacy, such a partnership is recommended. Instead, intimacy allows such an unnatural union to occur by providing the opposing characteristics a chance to reconcile their complete differences through the shared commonality of biological necessity and pleasure.

They interlock by the very nature that they oppose each other. What one is missing, the other provides, so that sexuality is expressed in revealing the unexpressed or unrealized parts of each party. When we discuss sexuality, we are primarily focusing on the experience of opposing genders interlocking, with each fulfilling the missing components. The missing components are the elements of each proponent which were overlooked by virtue of their subjective biases absorbed in the experience of life.

The Unexpressed and the External Realm

The unexpressed aspects can be seen as a lack of alignment with the external realm, to which one cannot self-identify. What is expressed, however, is reflected from the external world and allows for its innate observation. This refers to how sexuality can serve as a conduit for the sensibility of selfhood, through its external reflection. The differentiating aspects align with the dynamics of sexuality, especially when considering complex details that manifest in the representation of these dynamics.

The princess, as an example, offers sexuality a detailed experience of dignity and royal social depth. There is also the ability to perceive "princess-like" details within any sexual dynamic, which can manifest the representation akin to the actual princess. However, understanding what is "princess-like" requires retaining sentiments from previous frameworks. The unexpressed dynamic offers the opposing force, so that one who is royal will not need "princess-like" material.

One might counter this by suggesting that all elements should be incorporated without the necessity to rely on the opposing sexual party for these provisions. Yet, trying to expand beyond oneself by integrating the opposing sexual perspectives would cause a disengagement of the libido. The libido would be stranded, having the individual believe they have absorbed all sides of a perspective, rendering a third perspective unnecessary. This also applies when the libido serves no purpose because its holder has assumed a position of perfection, no longer needing intimacy, which would only dampen that position.

Immortality and the Libido

The notion of immortality is antithetical to the libido. To presume oneself already aligned with a future lineage, without acknowledging personal decay, undermines the reproductive system, which is predicated on imperfection and eventual disintegration. To assume an immortal stance, or one the psyche perceives as beyond the flaws and mortality intrinsic to life, weakens the impulse to engage with nature's response to finitude: sexuality.

The narcissist, according to Freud, still participates in a sexual dynamic, albeit from the perspective that the sexual object is in relation to themselves. This dynamic nonetheless requires the utilization of an opposing object in order to realize that internal reality.[23] Without a certain modesty toward the necessity of an external sexual object, even the narcissist ceases to function contained by a sexual framework and thus forfeits the designation. They behave as though they have already acquired the material worthy of exchange for a sexual dynamic. What results is not absolute narcissism, but rather the formation of immortal imagery.

Absolute narcissism still relies on an opposing sexual object for a certain realization of the self. It is common to critique the narcissist for its self-centric focus on sexuality or otherwise, while overlooking its beneficiaries, those who, by removing the third-party object of interest, go unquestioned. As the narcissist operates within the social realm, the dynamic opens a path for debasement, especially where the successor avoids active involvement and thus escapes scrutiny. Any thoughtful analysis of the social realm must acknowledge that the effects of such behavior persist, casting the narcissist in a parasitic role, an arrangement recognized as problematic in virtually any other context.

Participation in the social sphere is an inherent aspect of individual existence. When one ignores the symbolic and representational dimension embedded in people, others are reduced as problematic entities obstructing personal movement. Stripped of the sexual aspect, the social realm becomes depopulated of meaningful others, people are engaged as empty vessels, incapable of offering information or alteration. The entire interaction is an effort to affirm a pre-existing theory: that individuals contain no substantive material. Thus, others are dissolved into projections, imagined as complete yet devoid of relevance or vulnerability.

Such individuals perceive themselves as immortal, beyond susceptibility, and this translates materially as a state of totality composed of irrelevant substance. Yet what grants relevance, interest, and vitality to any person or thing are the very vulnerabilities and mortal limitations they bear, mortality attached to all things or aspects.

Philosophical Perspectives on Immortality and Sexuality

We find Greek philosophers were heavily focused on the concept of immortality, arguing that knowledge was the highest means of achieving it. They also critiqued the promiscuous nature of sexuality, especially in relation to the advanced individual. In their view, the libido was considered irrelevant; immortality, through knowledge, was not tied to reproduction.[24],[25]

However, in their pursuit of knowledge, particularly immortal knowledge, they neglected vulnerabilities, which led to a blind spot in their own assumptions. For a philosopher to roam the town and point out the vulnerabilities in others' conceptual realities would be a natural manifestation of this. It's as if the conceptual database isn't concerned with its vulnerabilities but with its perfection. The perfect conceptual realm, however, cannot be interacted with because it lacks the interactive properties of learning and teaching, both of which are vulnerabilities inherent in each data point.[26]

People were seen as devoid of material, their only flaw being the assumption that they possess it. The material they assume is the only point of interaction in any conceptual realm. The immortal perspective, granted to Greek intellectuals, allowed them to dismiss vulnerabilities as irrelevant within the conceptual realm. Yet it is these very vulnerabilities that make the conceptual, sexual, and social dynamics interesting. When everything is immortal, there is no dynamic; nothing is lost, and by extension, nothing is gained. To obtain more than immortality is impossible, and the complexity of material exists only because of the mortality of things. The rock is more immortal than humans or knowledge, yet it does not need or have the ability to interact. The complexity of the human mind, and consciousness in general, exists solely because of the mortal nature of existence. The celestial bodies, closer to immortality than most, lack the complexity found in human interaction because of this very issue.

From nature's perspective, one could postulate and behold the perfected position. Even if such a notion is illogical, the biological system follows a directive. It would suggest disengaging from promising sexual dynamics. If a human has perfected all necessary understandings, sexual union would hold no further assistance. This contrasts with a "perfectionist," who is overly concerned with their mistakes, quite the opposite of someone who perceives themselves as complete.

Imagine a perfectionist engaging with a potent libido, fully resolved to find weaknesses of personhood, which would manifest in the sexual union. The perfectionist by day would, by night, engage in a sexual dynamic revealing their vulnerabilities. In this sense, the sexual union becomes a means for teaching one's underdeveloped aspects. However, someone who assumes the role of both sides of a sexual union becomes detached from the libido, having nowhere left to learn. The libido, then, is contingent on recognizing one's vulnerabilities and the courage to seek development in one's counterpart.

These vulnerabilities must also be seen as extractable from the opposing dynamic. They must be placed upon the other, even if they are not yet fully understood. This requires the ability to perceive missing strands of material, which are passed on by to those in one's social circle who represent its entirety. The absolute vulnerability cannot be an area of exchange, as there is no preceding framework to absorb the material being offered. Rather, it is the partial understanding of the feminine within the masculine, and the masculine within the feminine, that is proposed to the opposing dynamic to complete their elemental understanding.

What is perceived as a weakness may be concealed through mental propositions, where the vulnerability is claimed as complete and incorporated within the persona, but not the psyche. One might even assume this development to be a dominant trait of their psyche, even though it is only attached to the persona. By asserting this proposition, the individual is removed from both perspectives; the vulnerability and its progression to wholeness and adaptation.

This is separate from the disarticulation of libido attachments. Engaging with a single perspective contains many layers of depth, and in some sense, such depth is inexhaustible. Thus, one must relinquish their original perspective to incorporate the opposing viewpoint into their psyche, gradually attenuating the original presence. Each perspective will displace the other, trapping them in an indeterminate limbo, where neither is truly experienced in its depth.

This dynamic is evident in any dialogical engagement where each party assumes a position. When both parties adopt the same stance, genuine conversation does not occur; instead, there is a reciprocal affirmation of each perspective. The primary goal of the conversation is not developmental change or insight, but rather the mutual recognition of existence. The existence of each participant is validated not only by their engagement but also by the recognition of the other's perspective, granting it a semblance of a more realistic form.

In such a scenario, the method of experiencing existence becomes cyclical. The interlocutor's engagement depends on their continuous concurrence with the other's perspective. This realization prevents them from experiencing a full validation of selfhood and perspective. Paradoxically, the one who assumes an antithetical stance can invoke such validation. By engaging with an opposing proponent who eventually adopts the perspective they initially posited, validation goes beyond circular conversational dynamics. The other enters the engagement without any predisposition to align with the proposition, and only through a profound understanding of its contents do they adopt the stance.

This also applies to a sexual union, which is not naturally experienced as a deep validation of existence because it involves dynamic opposition. The more self-reflective the union becomes, in an attempt to uncover its sexual material, the less validation of existence occurs. Since the partners are seemingly similar, they have no reason not to validate each other's existence. They are interacting from the same strand, devoid of diversity. What is opposite, however, creates the conditions for a meaningful union. This is why family members cannot fulfill the validation of one's selfhood; strangers outside the familial bond are required for self-recognition. The stranger's role can never be maintained by a family member because they embody a complete separation from familiarity, which enables them to oppose and evaluate one's existence and structure.

To truly learn what lies beyond, we must enter a domain, even if we already know more about it. For instance, we must live in a house to truly understand what "the outside" is. Without the house, we wouldn't experience it in the same way. "The outside" can only be fully understood from the perspective of being inside. Even though everyone has encountered the outside, they must mentally place themselves inside in order to grasp the depth of what is considered "outside." While one could theoretically assume all human roles, true understanding of each role comes only by taking it personally.

When raised in an enclosed space, one identifies the parameters of their existence based on the dimensions of that space. The entire reality framework is limited by that boundary. Once outside, it becomes apparent that the dimensions of selfhood cannot be projected onto such a vast space, as it lacks individuality and personhood. The outside, therefore, becomes a boundless realm that cannot contain selfhood.

The same is true for those raised only in the outside world. With the outside being the sole dimension of their reality, they will resist expanding their selfhood upon it. It is too vast for them to perceive any specificity or individuality, causing them to detach from external domains for self-reflection and existential perspective. Once they enter a private space, however, they will embrace the opportunity for personal reflection and conceptual boundaries. We cannot imagine an educated, developed person existing solely in the realm of the outside. They would never truly understand the narrower, more disciplined aspects of the conceptual world unless they have a private domain to map their developments.

Sensuality and Consciousness

Because humans are a composite of sexuality; sex, in its definable term, is a representation of all conscious dealings. Social dependency upon the environment for consciousness determines what arouses as sensual, to always align with present conscious flow.

This already finds many setbacks in logic, as one can encounter a sensual experience in whatever environment or state of psyche, to beat to the drum of its own music. However, the connection one has to the sensual department is the conversation at hand, that is, instead of the progress of sensuality in following the flow of consciousness.

We acknowledge such in the readily active activity of those heightened moments of life, which demand a form of sensuality in the displayed masculine and feminine representations. The clothed human will adhere to its form in the mitigation of sexual undertones, and the notion of style exempt from such will be in contempt by those who have a market to soften.

The most sensual will be the most consciously bound, and we can find such in the individual. The heightened sensual moments of life will be connected to what is deemed most primary by the individual. Sensuality towards the mother figure displays a primary attention to the occasion of the cradle. However, this does not prove to be the primary form of consciousness to which the individual is aligned but merely to the chosen perception, which is in opposition to that. This is the pity or condemnation we offer those who choose intimacy in following their own attachment to infantile sensitivities.

We acknowledge the role of those aspects of life but call to order a higher consciousness to which an intimate pattern would be aligned with the wholeness of personhood. Furthermore, in the case of the aristocratic mindset, or those in a position of structural consciousness, they will be compelled to follow the intimate partner not only for the wholeness of personhood but to preclude the wholeness of the environment which is represented in the partner. What is most primary in the environment should align with the market, which deems the top of the produce.

Part Two: Sexuality

The wholeness of the environment can be found in following sensitive aspects of sensuality, which will lead to a more lofty satisfaction of the sexual components. This satisfaction does not translate to a finality of climax but to the incorporation of all conscious flow into a primary measure. For the conscious flow is considerable, and to find a locale that can both include the dimension of all of its expanse while maintaining its center will be the most sensual. That very individual can easily disrupt this with mistaken masculine and feminine dynamics, which usually produce the paradoxical effect to which the most sensual experience can never be settled, satisfied, or even enjoyed.

The attempt at its enjoyment without the steady movement of the careful dynamics would make one leave the confines of sensuality and develop as another sexual experience of no high regard. Yet those who partake in the center of conscious flow in a given environment will handle the masculine-feminine dynamic with a heavy hand. Dealing with the ramifications for each sensual and sexual movement in the ripple effects of conscious flow will have any individual endearingly partake in each position.

The positioning will cause a lack of vision, inevitably leading to a failure to maintain a proper masculine-feminine dynamic. This decline will involve individuals in the most sensual environment, effectively blocking the reciprocity of that dynamic. Handling substantial movement takes an individual to an existential depth, supported only by a true form of philosophy. To the masculine, this philosophy is found in its details; to the feminine, in the existential appreciation of absolute femininity and the reception of that detailed depth. When we remove the masculine-feminine dynamic from sensuality, we become trapped in a feedback loop, as mentioned earlier. When sensuality arises for interaction, the failure of either the masculine or feminine dilutes its essence until the sexual finality loses its depth.

The Action of Sexuality

The action of sexuality is verily a negotiation between extraction and dispensation. Extraction motivates the dispensing properties to fulfill their emanation. To dispense is to release oneself of personal content by moving it toward its destination. Dispensation, however, lacks the ability to move the content forward, as it remains bound to the content in its stationary state.

Therefore, there is no true action of dispensing for the agent of dispensation, since engaging in that behavior would require detachment from the content.

Masturbation is an act of dispensation but involves being disconnected from the content to enable the dispensing behavior. This is why masturbation can be described as taking both roles in sexuality, or, more crudely, having sex with oneself. At any given moment during sexual activity, one can identify the roles of both dispenser and extractor, which may move from moment to moment. When the dispenser detaches from the content to fulfill the role of extractor, they dynamically request of the other party to take on the role of dispenser and connect to the content, making themselves ready for extraction.

To extract content, one initiates both a conceptual and physical process that incentivizes moving the content forward, with the ultimate aim of reaching climax. Extraction restricts the natural flow, pushing against the current. By halting the process, a dynamic tension ascends toward the content. This motivates the dispenser to first continue the natural flow and second, to oppose that tension by dispensing with greater force toward its destination. If extraction imposes too much restriction, then the intermediary step which allows the dispenser to respond by pushing forward will be entirely blocked, causing the process to halt, much like when a partner withdraws from the sexual act.

This interplay, restriction sending content inward (the inner motion) and allowance for free flow (the outer motion), is central to most sexual activity. The outer motion is the most sensitive aspect, as it can represent either a demand for extraction or an availability for dynamic exchange that enables extraction. The latter involves the dispenser reciprocating the restriction with increased thrust. The former, the demand for fulfillment by the extractor, is not the ultimate goal; rather, extraction of the content itself is. Though another person seems to be the destination of the content, it is actually the act of extraction that matters.

When the extractor treats their own fulfillment as the end product, they are not restricting the dispenser to enable extraction; rather, they are restricting the dispenser so that the extractor assumes the role of content. By restricting the content, they hope the dispenser will detach from the content and follow the extractor as the content source. However, from the viewpoint of the dispenser, they may be under the presumption that the extractor is the content but will lose sight of this once the restriction is done, and the activity spirits to the outer motion.

The only reason such an extractor tolerates the outer motion is that they recognize complete restriction will halt the sexual process. They also intuitively understand that it is the content that must be followed, as it is the true source of sexuality. For the dispenser, the outer motion can be confusing, the presumed content (the other party) is now moving away from the inner confines.

Why should the content separate from selfhood? This leads to another assumption: that the content is not external but within oneself. However, without an extractor to perform that function, caught between identifying as content and managing the outer space to ease restriction, this becomes impossible. Instead, one resorts to a kind of masturbation, extracting content through the body of the other, culminating in content to which they are not attached, due to the extraction role they must assume.

Sexual Diversity

Sexuality requires diversity because organic personhood cannot reproduce itself in a strict sense. For the individual to reproduce effectively, it must remove personhood from the occasion to allow for the capacity for more constructive development. The productive agent, that is the individual, does not require its own propagation by default, as there is no inherent benefit to having another copy of the same matter. The only way to convince the psyche and, subsequently, the organism of the necessity for such production is by incorporating a diverse array of new information along with diverse organisms that provide a nuanced edge to the production process.

Both the conceptual content and the organism involved in production are inherently diverse and idiosyncratic. When the conceptual information is the same, as in the case of an adopted sibling, we may have an engineered diverse organism, but the conceptual base lacks diversity. The attachment is found through a familial connection, a part of the psyche that gravitates toward similarity and which does not engage with the constitution through a habitual locale of universality.

The familial bond is already positioned against the diverse conceptual realm and its ascending social material. It has its unique purpose and objective, yet it is not the ideal candidate for conceptual diversity. For the psyche, the adopted sibling is treated as if a derivative of the same gene pool. Despite the best efforts of organic reality to present a different appeal, the conceptual realm may override a certain sense of reality, not with the effects of a highly abnormal production sequence, but sufficiently enough to disallow the full expression of sexuality that would enable diverse reproduction. Once the organism registers conceptual similarity, it withdraws from natural, organic sexuality in favor of a diluted version. In the absence of diversity, the organic expression resists fulfilling a sexual duty tied to a truly new gene pool.

True reproduction can be understood as occurring at the farthest edge of personhood, without crossing into adverse territory, as is sometimes observed in mammals. Codependency is a psychological manifestation of familial dependency, wherein the boundaries between individuals become indistinct. When this is the case, the sexual department will adjust with a demoted version of sexuality, as it presumes a non-diverse gene pool. This is the primary reason for the decline in libido often observed within marriage, as it functions under a political and social contract as a domestic union. This arrangement fosters a hyper-familial bond that tends to diminish sexuality, based on the assumption of a limited gene pool. We may wonder at the correlation, for in the actual realm, there can be a range of diversity in the organic material. To what reason, then, would the organic system take austere notation from the conceptual realm?

We can answer this conundrum with some interesting theories. The most traditional of these is that the sexual department is far more linked to the conceptual realm than to that of organic material. We find evidence of this, as primal elements of evolutionary development retain a demoted version of sexuality. The mammal, for example, is less engaged intellectually inclined in respect to their sexual activity, showing less regard for their own species, and it is normal to find sexual stimulation from higher life forms. Much of this could be attributed to the realm of sexual imagination, despite the regular organic function of sexuality running parallel to it. However, there may be more than just a parallel association between the two; the conceptual realm may not only serve as a lens to the dormant sexual department but also as a propagation of its contents.

This would also mean that when the conceptual realm lacks diversity, the organic matter produced for procreation will also lack diversity, regardless of the gene pool; as if the familial bond creates sexual stimulation that produces likeness in the gene pool. We partially acknowledge this, albeit with hesitation, when a couple begins to resemble each other physically or in mannerism. It is no great leap to assume that procreation overrides the gene pool to produce the average of both parents. The difference is that, while in a regular case reproduction draws from the entirety of both gene pools to create an optimal mix, when the gene pool has already been predetermined for the conceptual landscape, the offspring will be an average of that mixture, or worse, the elements most similar between the two. This results in reproduction as a copy of what has already been shared, producing the least diverse offspring possible.

Furthermore, the elements most similar between two individuals are often those in which each partner assume a lack of self-sufficiency, manifesting for the union as codependency. This results not only in lack of diversity but also suboptimal reproduction, where each partner assumes the elements which are so inhospitable that it must be validated by the other. This outcome is akin to incestuous reproduction, despite organic diversity being present. The lack of scientific findings in this area is due to persistent organic diversity, which masks the conceptual similarities which yield less optimal offspring. These conceptual overlaps are not flagged by traditional genetic screening, even though they may negatively affect reproductive outcomes.

We can draw a parallel with a research topic: birth order and its correlation with intelligence. Earlier-born children from the same parents are often found to be more astute. They are also more prone to substance abuse, which, as we've explained in other works, is a euphemism for an expanded existential state that does not connect with the social norms of society.[27] This data has been confirmed by Damian and Roberts (2015): "Regarding the link between birth order and intelligence, the results are much more consistent."[28]

We have research supporting the theory of conceptual diversity, where birth order's primary attribute is the conceptual diversity that initiates the relationship. Later siblings consistently result from a union that has declined in conceptual diversity. Familiarity over time generates conceptual similarity, resulting in a lack of diverse interaction. Though genetic diversity remains constant throughout the birth order, the key change lies in the conceptual shift from the first to later births. The first birth typically coincides with the early stage of the relationship, when partners do not yet correlate their conceptual realms, perceiving each other as distinct entities. Eventually, the conceptual realm alters this perception, assuming a genetic change, which leads to a union based on conceptual uniformity.

This underscores the conceptual vulnerability of replicating the organic situation under its own rules and assumptions. It presumes that continuity equates to a lack of diversity, with memory serving as a marker of similarity, even though the organic state remains unchanged. Yet we still observe a tangible development in later births, where conceptual discernment affects sexual diversity despite a consistent organic reality. The scientific community has not explored this area thoroughly, though birth order research is a starting point for observing shifts in conceptual perception among minor variables, such as the attentiveness of parental care for firstborns.

Because the research of Bjerkedal (2007) included many cases unaffected by parental preferential treatment, we can overlook that variable. Within that study, a notable correlation emerges: *the spacing of the birth order*. "A short spacing, less than 1 year between first and second births, appears to give the largest difference in standardized score [the largest decline in intelligence scores]. With more than 5 years between first and second births and between second and third, differences in scores appear to diminish."

They fail to mention the uptrend from six to eight-plus years, especially in the spacing between the second and third siblings, which is crucial to our study. This spacing reflects the availability of conceptual diversity at different stages of the union. Less than a year between births prevents the conceptual realm from registering the organic diversity still at play. Extending to five years, the perception diminishes slightly, as the extended duration presumes a detachment from the union itself. The uptrend of six to eight years reflects the final appropriation of the relationship as one to be entertained, while the spacing presumes conceptual diversity.

Another approach is the simpler explanation that the libido will not activate if the conceptual realm does not grant custody to sexual expression, having assumed the union to be lacking diversity. If, for any reason, we can bypass this conceptual limitation by accessing a heightened libido, then the production will correlate with the actual organic material and its respective diversity. This would mean that diversity does not correlate with any happenstance of the conceptual realm, only the imaginative conceptual realm attributes such to lack diversity.

This is difficult to accept, because the conceptual realm is so active in sexuality that it is hard to believe it has no effect on the sexual material. When the libido is stimulated with medicinal substances, the sexual department is granted access, and the conceptual claim of universality fades away. The selection of genes becomes systemic, and the relationship no longer affects the outcome. Our aversion to sexual relations with an adopted sibling is symbolic, an echo of the taboo of incest, but would not inherently result in suboptimal offspring due to conceptual similarity alone. We do not retain evidence of offspring being suboptimal solely because of conceptual uniformity.

The libido can be perceived as an elementary part of the organic system, one that is not available to conceptual sexuality. The only reason the conceptual realm can entertain sexuality is that it has access to the whole organic system. The fact that sexuality is a subtext of the organic system becomes magnified when the conceptual realm mirrors the entire system; almost as if there is shame surrounding sexuality, being an infantile remnant of evolutionary development. This may help explain the shame often associated with sexuality as a primal shame, rooted in early evolutionary stages.

What is elementary becomes highly potent in modeling processes; what appears to be the fantastical realm of sexuality may simply be a translation mechanism that exaggerates its importance. Modeling follows the sequence of the mirrored object. Unlike the complexity of the object itself, the modeling process extracts only the stimulating aspects that follow a linear function. Thus, modeling is a linear extraction of data points that track from an infantile origin to a present form, granting the illusion that the object has been fully incorporated. First, it perceives the object as a system by tracing a developmental sequence, and second, it identifies the most potent aspects along that path, assuming that each stage encompasses the entire system.

The organic realm may not prioritize sexuality, viewing it as a precursor to more complex developmental functions. The organic realm may, in fact, be trending toward immortality or extended life, where latent sexuality stands in contrast. Nonetheless, we must deal with the reality that such a translation has already occurred. Despite the organic disapproval of sexuality, as seen in its frequent association with disgust, the conceptual realm elevates the sexual realm to a position of supreme importance. Any attempt to convince the conceptual realm otherwise would be in vain, for the structural modeling of the organic system cannot be altered, and sexuality remains central. Any effort to dismantle sexuality as a subject would come at the cost of the entire psychic structure, a point early psychoanalysts observed.[29]

An alternative, albeit less convincing position is the opposite: that the organic system is entirely at the mercy of sexuality, perceiving the life form as destined to propagate externally, with sexuality as the mechanism. In this view, the entire existential state is bonded with the sexual department, viewing selfhood as dependent on reproduction. This seems implausible: what would be the purpose of an expanded conceptual realm if its only aim was to enlarge sexuality? Especially considering that the conceptual realm more often distracts from sexual aims than supports them. If we were to construct a device to enlarge sexuality, the psyche would likely be the last candidate for that task.

We might further postulate that the psyche balances sexuality with intelligence to produce offspring capable of sustaining continued sexuality. But for what purpose would such offspring exist, only to continue sexual reproduction? If the goal is reproductive quality, the department best suited for that is not the conceptual realm. As mentioned, conceptual attributes have only a minor effect on sexual outcomes. The healthy gene pool remains the primary factor, an element the conceptual realm has little direct access to. We might even view the psyche as an anti-sexual device, designed to mask organic vulnerabilities and potentially to replace procreation with internal production.

Sexual Representation and the Limits of Organic Function

A sexual thought that engages with the organic sexual function is only made possible through representation within consciousness. It's tempting to assume the opposite; that sexuality, being present throughout nature, must function organically, with consciousness merely interacting with it or remaining uninvolved, but never serving as its origin. This assumption stems from the belief that lower life forms do not engage in representation, viewing it as an exclusive trait of consciousness.

Animals that exhibit a sexual response to human forms do so because those forms represent something for them. They are not sexually animated purely by organic function; rather, it's their mental capacity that constructs an image of sexuality. This image acts as a representation, perhaps not sophisticated by human standards, but still a subliminal form of imagination that cannot be entirely reduced to organic function. Sexuality in lower life forms is also a form of representation, though it doesn't lead to attraction at the human level because it lacks comprehension.

Even though sexuality appears to be organic, the fact that one is not always sexually active, unlike hunger, suggests that consciousness does not simply suppress a constant sexual drive. Instead, it never generates such in the first place. This is why any sexually motivated thought must increase contained by consciousness and its representations. However, representation alone does not sustain sexuality in its entirety. A picture may be drawn to entice interaction, but the interaction itself can still fail. For example, the fashion industry creates elaborate portrayals of sexuality, which could be considered a form of sexual representation. However, this representation doesn't always translate into everyday sexual interaction. A recurring theme emerges: one may adhere to sexual representation while simultaneously avoiding direct sexual engagement.

Beyond the discomfort of engaging with sexual representation in a physical way, there is also a loss of that representation when it transitions into domestic and interactive reality. However, excessive avoidance can prevent one from properly representing sexuality, thereby diminishing the sexual significance once associated with a fashion piece. Therefore, a proper degree of sexual interaction is necessary to maintain the ability to represent sexuality as a theme. Yet, at the moment of direct interaction, the representation fades, and sexuality becomes domesticated.

The Oedipus Complex and Search for Sexual Representation

If we are to look at the Oedipus complex through a different framework, we arrive at varying results. Instead of perceiving the will of the child as a sexual inclination toward a familial complex, we must view sex in isolation as a mechanism that does not conform to the limited parameters of the parental structure.

Although parents are the preoccupation of children, at least small children, this should not be viewed as a direct interpretation but rather as a means to an end. The end, which is by no means confined to the parents, arises because the child is seeking universal sex, as its organic members which facilitate the process do not distinguish a specific sexual target but instead manifest all things sexual.

Of course, early psychoanalysts noted a direct linkage to the parental figure, and while we do not dispute this, we assert that it is not the complete analysis when all factors are considered. It is also worth noting that this will not be a complete analysis, but rather another perspective that offers answers as to why this sexual theory did not gain traction in later psychological research.

When we view sex in a wholesome manner, the first question we must ask regarding the child is: what environment is the child involved in? It is not in concern with finding the sexual object right away, for our theory leads away from the parent, leaving no room for preliminary stages.

First and foremost, sex is a tool for one to gain a feminine or masculine experience to the nth degree. It cannot be said that sex is simply for the male to experience female tendencies, nor solely for the female; rather, the male is to discover what is most efficient within him, that is, the complex female tendencies that can be embodied through sexual fantasies.

This means that when parental figures do not provide that objective, when each figure fails to offer that result, we either have a reversal of the Oedipus complex or a child who does not see the sexual object contained by the parents. Instead, the child is primarily asexual, as the stimulating effect of granting a feminine or masculine experience is lacking, and, in truth, the child is sent in search of an environment that provides that nuance absent in the parents.

Already at a young age, the child notices the sexual incompetence of the parental figure and finds no refuge in them. For this reason alone, the child does not receive an adequate formation of child-to-parent development; if they do not meet sexual demands, surely they are not proficient in loving them, and all attempts are ultimately futile.

When a child seeks a primary sexual object outside the failed attempt with the parental figure, it is an effort to replace that figure, not merely as a semblance, but with something better. The difference here is that the child who has fully developed within the Oedipus complex will also replace figures with their adult spouse, concurrently mirroring that childhood development. In cases of inadequate parental sexual imbuement, the child prematurely replaces the figure so that adulthood finds them never fully satisfied in the sexual department. This is because they remain in doubt as to whether the sexual object meets standards that were never clearly defined.

Thus, we have a scenario in which the child never becomes sexually attached to the parental figure and instead becomes fixated on the environment to provide an adequate sexual representation that meets a certain criterion. Neurosis emerges here in a different form. Instead of the neurotic opposing the superego's demand, they find themselves unable to organize their desire in accordance with their perceptual experience. In doing so, they amplify their desire and become neurotic, not as a conflict between the superego and the unconscious, but because the unconscious recognizes its own inadequacy, prompting the superego to demand an experience adequate only in perceptual terms.

We can see how this leads to a more socially unacceptable inclination, wherein the child or adult becomes fixated on the environment to locate their unconscious desire and shape it so that it may be considered wholesome.

There is another aspect concerning the context in which the parental figure is embedded, for sexual competency is viewed as a representation. If parental figures are embedded in an environment of advanced civilization, then the mother or father is seen as both a manifestation and a representation of that environment. Despite their level of feminine or masculine experience, they will highlight whatever subtleties they possess, influenced by the environment, which can then become part of the child's object.

When the environment does provide that assistance, we must examine the parental figure, which may not exhibit feminine or masculine traits sufficient for the child. In such cases, the parents also lack a fully developed sense of sexuality because they have distanced themselves from civilization. The child will then embark on a sexual hunt within the realm where civilization is most effective in providing an adequate sexual object, having experienced a lack of stimulation in that arena. The child acknowledges that there is something more, noticing the innate dependency of the parent upon the environment.

For if they are simply sequestered in a forest, the primordial family reemerges, and the parents become self-reliant for all matters related to sexuality; a situation the child finds wholesome, as it does not reveal a lineage of superior sexuality beyond the parental figure.

However, the Oedipus complex does not presume domination in every primordial family, but only in those that exhibit a conscious sentiment to which sexuality is tied, such that the traits of femininity and masculinity are merely roles for conscious interaction. Without a highly developed conscious layer, sexuality takes a backseat, and the range of potential objects is limited, resulting in neurosis, unless there is an awareness of a consciousness beyond the parental figure, rendering the unconscious desire inadequate.

Further Reading

Psychoanalysis and Sexual Theory
Freud, Sigmund. Three Essays on the Theory of Sexuality. Translated by James Strachey. New York: Basic Books, 2000.
Freud, Sigmund. Three Essays on the Theory of Sexuality. In The Standard Edition of the Complete Psychological Works of Sigmund Freud, Vol. 7. London: Hogarth Press, 1953.
Freud, Sigmund. Introductory Lectures on Psychoanalysis (1916–1917). Standard Edition, Vols. 15–16. London: Hogarth Press.
Freud, Sigmund. Instincts and Their Vicissitudes (1915). Standard Edition, Vol. 14.
Freud, Sigmund. Beyond the Pleasure Principle (1920). Standard Edition, Vol. 18.
Freud, Sigmund. The Ego and the Id (1923). Standard Edition, Vol. 19.
Freud, Sigmund. The Dissolution of the Oedipus Complex (1924). Standard Edition, Vol. 19.
Freud, Sigmund. Female Sexuality (1931). Standard Edition, Vol. 21.
Freud, Sigmund. New Introductory Lectures on Psycho-Analysis (1933), Lecture XXXI: The Dissection of the Psychical Personality. Standard Edition, Vol. 22.
Freud, Sigmund. Civilization and Its Discontents (1930). Standard Edition, Vol. 21.

Biology, Evolution, and Behavior
Buss, David M. Evolutionary Psychology: The New Science of the Mind. 6th ed. New York: Routledge, 2019.
Sapolsky, Robert. Behave: The Biology of Humans at Our Best and Worst. New York: Penguin Press, 2017.
Seligman, Martin E. P. Helplessness: On Depression, Development, and Death. San Francisco: W. H. Freeman, 1975.
Bjerkedal, T., Kristensen, P., Skjeret, G. A., & Brevik, J. I. "Intelligence Test Scores and Birth Order among Young Norwegian Men." Intelligence 35, no. 6 (2007).
Damian, R. I., & Roberts, B. W. "Settling the Debate on Birth Order and Personality." Proceedings of the National Academy of Sciences 112, no. 46 (2015): 14119–14120.

Sexuality, Anthropology, and Culture
Diamond, Milton. "Sexual Behavior in Pre-Contact Hawai'i: A Sexological Ethnography." Journal of Sex Research, 2023.
Marshall, Sexual Behavior in Pre-Contact Hawai'i. 2004.
Stillman, Amy, citing Lilikalā Kameʻeleihiwa. Native Land and Foreign Desires: Pehea Lā E Pono Ai? Honolulu: Bishop Museum Press, 1992.
12 Years a Slave. Directed by Steve McQueen. 2013.

Gender, Philosophy, and Social Theory
De Beauvoir, Simone. The Second Sex. Translated by Constance Borde and Sheila Malovany-Chevallier. New York: Vintage Books, 2011.
Weininger, Otto. Sex and Character. 1903.

Fineman, Martha Albertson. The Autonomy Myth: A Theory of Dependency. New York: The New Press, 2004.

Classical Philosophy and Literature

Plato. Apology. Translated by Benjamin Jowett. New York: Dover Publications, 2004.

Plato. Phaedo. Translated by G. M. A. Grube. Indianapolis: Hackett Publishing Company, 1997.

Aristotle. Nicomachean Ethics. Translated by W. D. Ross. Chicago: University of Chicago Press, 2002.

Aristotle. Poetics.

Rousseau, Jean-Jacques. Confessions. Written 1765–1770, published 1782–1789.

Shakespeare, William. Sonnet 116. In The Complete Works of William Shakespeare. Oxford University Press, 1988.

Notes

1 Sigmund Freud, Three Essays on the Theory of Sexuality, trans. James Strachey (New York: Basic Books, 2000), 22; Gay, P. (1988). Freud: A life for our time. W. W. Norton & Company.

2 Simone de Beauvoir, The Second Sex, translated by Constance Borde and Sheila Malovany-Chevallier (New York: Vintage Books, 2011), p. 52.

3 Isaacson, Walter. Steve Jobs. New York: Simon & Schuster, 2011.

4 12 Years a Slave.

5 Diamond, M. (2023). Sexual behavior in pre-contact Hawai'i: A Sexological ethnography. Journal of Sex Research.

6 Buss, D. M. (2019). Evolutionary Psychology: The New Science of the Mind (6th ed.). Routledge.

7 Collias, N. E., & Collias, E. C. (1973). An experimental study of the mechanisms of nest building in a weaverbird. The Auk, 90(1), 136–151.

8 Weininger, Otto. Sex and Character (1903).

9 Freud, S. (1905). Three Essays on the Theory of Sexuality (J. Strachey, Trans.). In J. Strachey (Ed.), The Standard Edition of the Complete Psychological Works of Sigmund Freud (Vol. 7, pp. 123–243). London: Hogarth Press.

10 Freud, S. (1916–1917). Introductory Lectures on Psychoanalysis (J. Strachey, Trans.). In J. Strachey (Ed.), The Standard Edition of the Complete Psychological Works of Sigmund Freud (Vols. 15–16). London: Hogarth Press.

11 Martha Albertson Fineman, The Autonomy Myth: A Theory of Dependency (New York: The New Press, 2004), 31.

12 Freud, S. (1923). The Ego and the Id. In The Standard Edition of the Complete Psychological Works of Sigmund Freud, Vol. 19, trans. James Strachey. London: Hogarth Press.
See also Freud, S. (1924). The Dissolution of the Oedipus Complex. Standard Edition, Vol. 19; and Freud, S. (1931). Female Sexuality. Standard Edition, Vol. 21.

13 Freud, S. (1923). The Ego and the Id. In The Standard Edition of the Complete Psychological Works of Sigmund Freud, Vol. 19, trans. James Strachey. London: Hogarth Press.
See especially sections on the relative autonomy of the id, the ego's mediating function, and the superego as an internalized authority rather than a self-sustaining regulator.
See also Freud, S. (1933). New Introductory Lectures on Psycho-Analysis, Lecture XXXI, The Dissection of the Psychical Personality. Standard Edition, Vol. 22.

14 Robert Sapolsky, Behave: The Biology of Humans at Our Best and Worst (2017)

15 (T Bownes, E C O'Gorman)

16 Seligman, M. E. P. (1975). Helplessness: On depression, development, and death. W. H. Freeman.

17 Amy Stillman, citing Lilikalā Kameʻeleihiwa, Native Land and Foreign Desires: Pehea Lā E Pono Ai? (Honolulu: Bishop Museum Press, 1992).

18 Marshall, Sexual Behavior in Pre-Contact Hawai'i, 2004, p. 37.

19 Freud, S. (1920). Beyond the pleasure principle. The International Psycho-Analytical Library.

20 Aristotle, Poetics.

21 Jean-Jacques Rousseau, Confessions (French: Les Confessions), written between 1765 and 1770, published posthumously in 1782–1789. Although potently sensual, the manner he talks about the act is with disgust.

22 Shakespeare, William. Sonnet 116. The Complete Works of William Shakespeare. Oxford University Press, 1988.

23 Freud, Sigmund. Three Essays on the Theory of Sexuality, 1953.

24 Plato. (1997). Phaedo (G. M. A. Grube, Trans.). Hackett Publishing Company. (Original work published ca. 360 BCE)

25 Aristotle. Nicomachean Ethics. Translated by W. D. Ross, The University of Chicago Press, 2002. (Original work published ca. 340 BCE)

26 Plato. (2004). Apology (B. Jowett, Trans.). Dover Publications. (Original work published ca. 399 BCE)

27 Bjerkedal, T., Kristensen, P., Skjeret, G. A., & Brevik, J. I. (2007). Intelligence test scores and birth order among young Norwegian men (conscripts) analyzed within and between families.

28 Damian RI, Roberts BW. Settling the debate on birth order and personality. Proc Natl Acad Sci U S A. 2015 Nov 17;112(46):14119-20. doi: 10.1073/pnas.1519064112. Epub 2015 Oct 30. PMID: 26518507; PMCID: PMC4655556.

29 Freud, S. (1905). Three Essays on the Theory of Sexuality. In The Standard Edition of the Complete Psychological Works of Sigmund Freud, Vol. 7, trans. James Strachey. London: Hogarth Press.

Freud, S. (1915). Instincts and Their Vicissitudes. Standard Edition, Vol. 14.

Freud, S. (1920). Beyond the Pleasure Principle. Standard Edition, Vol. 18.

Freud, S. (1930). Civilization and Its Discontents. Standard Edition, Vol. 21.

www.ingramcontent.com/pod-product-compliance
Lightning Source LLC
Chambersburg PA
CBHW061753120626
46550CB00005B/1978